SEARCHING FOR SOUL

SEARCHING FOR SOUL

Reg Stickings

First published in 2008
by SAF Publishing
First edition

SAF Publishing Ltd.
149 Wakeman Road, London.
NW10 5BH
ENGLAND

email: info@safpublishing.co.uk
www.safpublishing.co.uk

ISBN: 978 0 946719 87 7 Paperback edition

Cover design and photography: Alan Cottee
All photographs from the author's collection.

In some cases it has not proved possible to ascertain or trace original illustration
copyright holders, and the publishers would be grateful to hear from the photographers
concerned.

All lyrics quoted are for review, study or critical purposes.

The publishers and the author would like to thank Nicole Andrews, Jackie Fitzgerald,
and Alison Parkes. This book would not have been possible without their invaluable
contributions.

A CIP catalogue record for this book is available from the British Library.

Printed in England by the Cromwell Press, Trowbridge, Wiltshire.

Dedicated to the memory of
"me Mum" and "me Dad"
Colleen Joan and Raymond Harold Stickings
"You get out of life, what you put in."

Contents

Foreword

Now, when you struggle through your time at school with reading and writing, you might think that the last thing anybody should attempt is to write a book!

Like many of you reading this, I have contemplated a fanciful thought of 'one day, when I get the time, I am going to write a book' and that is as far as most of us get. However, for Reg this dream has now become a reality. It has not been easy, but his powers of recollection are amazing, even down to the details of conversations that took place over thirty years ago.

Reg is a storyteller! Whether we are out for a night 'souling', thumbing through records, meeting people for the first time, having a meal or just on a visit to each other's houses, there is always a story. The concept of a book came out of the blue one day about seven years ago. Once Reg had decided to give it a go, he made time to create this book and received nothing but support from all of his family and his many friends.

This book will not try to influence you in any religious or social way, nor will it attempt to deflect you from your musical preference. It will tell you a story of ordinary folk, growing up, their passion for music, the search for things that maybe weren't understood at the time, the highs and lows that life deals out and the love and appreciation of family and friends. It is a story that most of us can and will relate to in parts; you may see yourself or someone you know featured in this book—the names may be different but the experiences and characters will be there. I guess to sum it up, it's a diary about life and we have all experienced that.

I have known Reg for some forty years now and in reading these memoirs, I even had a tear or two at times and I was there! We have been friends for a long time and although we went our separate ways for a while, our passion and love of music has drawn us back together and so the search goes on.

Reg knows a lot of people and a lot of people know Reg. He always has a big smile for anyone and everyone and when meeting him for the first time you feel as though you have known him for years. Even when he is hurting inside, outwardly the smile is still there to cheer up everyone else. And like we all have had to bear from time to time, Reg has had his fair share of hurt.

There is no doubt in my mind that you will enjoy Reggie's story, even if your views on music, fashion, football and the rest differ. It doesn't matter, just read it and accept it for what it is—life.

Enjoy,
Yogi

Introduction

I'm sorry I'm late but when I tell you the reason, I'm sure you will forgive me. You see I've just come back from a concert you won't believe. Who I have just seen? Isaac Hayes at the Shepherd's Bush Empire, and what a tidy little venue. If you can imagine an old Victorian theatre with not one, but three horseshoe-shaped balconies covered in them old plastered-type patterns, and where you normally find the stall seats they had all been removed revealing an old magnificent dance floor. In my opinion it was quite a special little place

And you'll never guess how we got the tickets; me ole mate Alan Cottee won them by answering a question on the radio, which wasn't hard to do as the question was: "What film theme did Isaac Hayes write the sound track for?" I mean even yours truly could have answered that. It was *Shaft* wasn't it?

Anyway before we start my story I've got to tell you how brilliant Isaac Hayes was. I have been to many concerts in my lifetime and seen many Soul artists perform as you will soon find out, but this man was something really special. The band and the backing singers were playing some typical Hayes music; heavy bass, trumpets, violins, oboes the lot. The sound was just like listening to a full-blown orchestra, although most of the sound I was hearing was being played by just three guys using seven synthesisers. Apart from the drummer, bass player and electric guitarist, there were three backing singers; two girls; one black and one white, and a black fella. Then all of a sudden the man in question shuffled onto the stage just like a God. The only time I've ever seen an artist of this calibre look so powerful was in the Rainbow Theatre in Finsbury Park, when Stevie Wonder walked out onto the stage wearing an afghan coat with dry ice hiding his feet giving the appearance of standing on a cloud.

Although Issac Hayes looked a very powerful man, you could see how frail he really was by the way he shuffled towards the spare synthesisers. I know it has taken me a long time to see this great man perform, as nowadays he must be in his late sixties, but it was well worth the wait. Isaac was wearing a bright red Kurtas Pyjama type garment just like Muslim gents wear and a pair of large sunglasses. Isaac started playing the spare synthesisers along with the band, and after a good couple of minutes he opened his mouth and started to sing. As soon as this happened, them old tingles went straight up my back and down my arms, what a voice it was just like on his recorded records, no I would go as far as say it was better than on his records. Isaac only sang about seven or eight 'choons', as most of his songs last about six or seven minutes each, instead of the norm two-and-a-half to five.

There were four Isaac Hayes records that absolutely blew me away. The first was his version of 'Walk On By', then of course was 'Joy' which really got the audience going, but what I was about to witness next was far beyond anything I'd ever seen before. The white backing singer walked from where she was standing towards Isaac Hayes and sat down beside him. Half of the band started to play Aretha Franklin's 'Say A Little Prayer' then with such passion the white lady starts to sing; "*The moment I wake up, before I put on my makeup.*"

When the lady gets to the word "*makeup*", Isaac Hayes starts singing and playing "*By the time I get to Phoenix*"; both singers intermingled the two songs to perfection. Well in my time I thought I'd seen it all but I have never seen anything like this in my life and I doubt if I will ever again. If there is anyone in this world who could get me this recording on a seven inch piece of vinyl I'd definitely want to know about it as it was the best live performance I have ever seen.

I know you want me to get on with what I have sat down to do, but just let me tell you about this bit. When the white singer went back and stood between the other backing singers, Isaac Hayes gingerly stood up, steadying himself by placing one hand on the side of the synthesisers, then shuffled to the centre of the stage. With his back to the audience he started to conduct the band. When this all-time brilliant piece of music reached boiling point, Isaac Hayes turned round to face the audience and started to sing:

Who is the man that would risk his neck for his brother man…
Shaft ….
You're darn right…

Need I say any more?

Right I'll just have a sip of me cup of tea, sharpen up the pencil and get started……..

Chapter 1

Kids' Stuff!

Hi guys. My name is Reg. I am currently 53 years old and this is my story about searching for Soul. I am not special, I have never done anything unique, but my story just relates my life, my experiences and my music.

I count myself to be a very lucky person. I have had a wonderful life and met thousands of lovely people. I sincerely hope you enjoy reading this book as much as I enjoyed writing it. For some of you, parts of my story will be very familiar, to others it may appear strange, but it is all real.

I was born in Hemel Hempstead on St George's Day, 1954, the 23rd of April. My Dad worked at Rotax, where they made aircraft components and me Mum worked at the local paper mill—John Dickinson. My Dad's job came with a council house if you were prepared to move out of London to this new town called Hemel Hempstead. We didn't have a lot. Mum and Dad worked hard, and I was the eldest of three—me (Reg), my brother Geoff and my little sister Jackie. Whilst Mum and Dad were working during the day, we stayed at my Gran's house.

When I was about 10 years old, Mum and Dad let me stay at my cousin's house in Sittingbourne in Kent, for the best part of the summer holiday. It was brilliant. I learned to sea-fish and shoot. Hand picking hops were all but finished, but cherry picking was still going on and if we helped my cousin's Nan with the cherries, she would give us some pocket money. To raise more money, we tried to sell the fish we had caught, and when we were older we dived off the jetty for pennies thrown into the sea by holidaymakers at Brighton. When I look back in life, this game of survival was a good learning curve for the future, as most of us have Champagne tastes and Lemonade pockets, especially when it comes to buying rare records.

My cousins, Vivian, Richard and Kevin, their Mum and Dad (Auntie Ruby and Uncle Viv) were true rural folk. Uncle Viv worked on a building site as a carpenter. If he got home early enough, my cousins and I would dive into his dormobile and persuade him to take us to Dreamland in Margate. But it wasn't the amusement park that I was interested in. At the entrance to the park, there was a surf-type bar called the 'Bali Hi' where the most amazing music was being played. Young as I was, I loved sitting outside listening to the sounds....

Another time, the whole family was in Kent for the August Bank Holiday, when we heard that it had all kicked off in Brighton. I looked at the *East Kent Gazette* at the pictures of the Mods and Rockers, then looked at my Auntie Carol... She had a 'bob' haircut, like the French singer, Mireille Mathieu ('Sometimes You Make Me Cry') and a sort of pencil cut dress. When comparing her looks to the pictures in the paper, I suddenly realised that Auntie Carol was a Mod!!

Back in Hemel Hempstead, on numerous occasions I asked her to take me out with her, but there was no way that Auntie Carol was having a kid hanging around when she was out with her mates. But, when she was out in the evenings, my Gran allowed me into her room. On a wood and plastic Sixties style table was what you might call a vanity case. It was like a round hatbox with a flat edge on one side and a handle opposite. I would dearly love to own it these days, because inside the box was a little record player that you could either plug in or use with batteries. I was always playing her records. They were a bit 'charty'—Gerry and The Pacemakers, The Animals, Cilla Black.... I am surprised I didn't get bored—Auntie Carol only had 15 records!

At this time of life, things were looking sweet in 1966. Liverpool FC, my team had won the First Division; England had won the World Cup and I only had one year to go to get into the local youth club.

The big stores ran a club card, where you paid so much per week and when you had saved enough, you could go and buy some clothes. Aunty Ruby in Kent was in the 'Provi Club' or the 'Pru', my Mum was in the 'Co-op' but this was no good to me because I wanted Levis. It took me ages to convince my Mum that this was the way to dress if you wanted to look the part. I was twelve-and-a-half when I got my first pair of Levis and yes, my dad did take the pee when I got out of the bath with blue legs as they had to be shrunk to size on you. Shortly after, followed the crew-neck pullover, and if you could afford a pair of world-cup trainers you were top dollar—cool as cucumber!

The big day arrived—my 13th birthday.

I took half an hour to get ready. As I strolled round to the Youth Club in Bennetts End, I had tremendous butterflies in my stomach and guess what, because I was so small, the guy on the door didn't believe my age and wouldn't let me in!

On the way back home, a girl said, "Well you look the part, but what's up?"

I told her it was my 13th birthday, but they wouldn't let me in the youth club. She walked along with me for a while.

When we got to my house, she said, "I know who you are, you're little Reg. Come home with me while I get ready—I'll get you in. My name's Pippa, Pippa Brewster."

When we got back to Pippa's house, I could see she was a young lady with quite a lot of authority.

She said, "I'm not having it Mum, if the boy is old enough, why don't they let him in?" Then she said, "Right, I'm ready Reg." Walking up the road, Pippa said laughingly, "If he doesn't let you in this time, I'll tell him you're my boyfriend!"

I thought I'd won the pools! I wasn't going up the club on my own, I was going with one of the 'faces'; a lovely looking modette as well. What a result!!

When we got to the club, there were two scooters outside, and the guy on the door didn't say a word when Pippa said, "Two please."

The club was a right dive, but the people were great. I took a bit of banter.

"Did you fetch your bird up on your scooter, son?"

"Do you want a lift up onto the barstool?"

But it was all in good jest. I had a half-crown on me. Pippa and I sat at the bar. They sold 7Up, Coca-Cola and a drink called Pepsi—I asked

Pippa about Pepsi and she said it was the same as Coke, so I bought a couple of Pepsis, two Milky Ways and still had some change!

Out of the corner of my eye I noticed a chap with a cream box with a lift-off lid—a bit different from Auntie Carol's record player—twice the size, with a long centre stem, which you could load up with about eight records. When one record finished, another fell down and the arm moved all by itself. On the arm, above the needle was a sticking plaster with a ha'penny on it.

I asked why it was there and the chap said, "More weight. The records are shit, they haven't been looked after, the extra weight stops them jumping. If ever you can afford records, look after them. Buy an 'Emitex' cleaning cloth, especially if they are rare."

I found out what he meant by rare later on in life—big time! Then the record kicked in—a guitar start.

In a second, I said, "'House Of The Rising Sun', by The Animals."

"You know your stuff, son," he said.

Well most of the sounds/records were the same as Auntie Carol's. Then all of a sudden, a brilliant record came on with fantastic words— *"Give me a ticket for an aeroplane, ain't got time to take a fast train."*

"What's this?" I asked.

Pippa said, "Do you like this one Reg? It's 'The Letter' by The Box Tops. (It was on a Stateside label.) It's soul music," but in the same breath, she knocked me for six, "I've got some bad news for you, Reg. The youth club is closing. I think it's going to have a re-furb. I doubt if we'll come any more. We don't like change, it won't be the same."

"Oh no," I thought. All this time I had waited to be a member of a youth club and now it was closing.

Chapter 2

Late Sixties

During most of the late sixties, I followed my beloved football team, Liverpool, up and down the country. The Beatles were dominating the record charts. The music programmes were *Juke Box Jury* and *Ready Steady Go* and if you wanted any kind of colour on your telly, you stuck an old Lucozade wrapper on the screen. Flower Power was just around the corner, and there was still no youth club. My Dad made me a crystal wireless with headphones, and on a good night you could pick up Radio Caroline—a good station, but not much soul music.

When I was 14, in 1967, my Dad took us surfing at Woolacombe. This was where I bought my first piece of vinyl. No 1 in the charts was 'All You Need Is Love' by The Beatles, but the record that I purchased was 'Don't Sleep In The Subway' by Petula Clark, not quite soul music, but a good tune. On the campsite, was a small youth club. The club was a lot smarter than Bennetts End, but the people weren't. There wasn't a mod in sight. They looked like a bunch of hippies with beads around their wrists and necks, and sun-bleached long hair. They called themselves "Surf Bums". The small club sold Coca Cola, 7-Up and a drink called Vimto—a reddy colour. Auntie 'hands off my record player' Carol drank a fruit cocktail called Pimms No 1 or Babycham.

Back in Hemel Hempstead, hippies were springing up as fast as the flowers in the back gardens but the cool kids were wearing their favourite football team's tops, Levis, crew neck jumpers and basketball boots or trainers. The little kids' shoes were Jumping Jacks or Wayfinders with animal footprints on the soles and a compass in the heel, just in case you got lost so that you could find your way home—way finders!

On the evening of December 11th 1967, I strolled down Great Whites Road where Pippa lived and as I turned the corner, I saw Pippa.

"Alright Pip?" I asked.

"No not really" she replied, "My favourite soul singer died yesterday."

"Which one?" I asked,

"Otis Redding," said Pip. "He was killed in a plane crash."

It wasn't until over a year later that I realised what soul fans had lost—probably one of the greatest soul singers ever. I now own a couple of Otis Redding singles. One is 'Dock Of The Bay', the other's 'Try A Little Tenderness'. Oh, and I also have 'Mr Pitiful' on a re-issue, but that is it, because at the time of my life when I could finally afford to buy records, I was well into Reggae and Tamla Motown.

During the following year, I spent most of my time kicking my football around over the park. This was where I met Stan Brewster (Pippa's younger brother), Tony Lock and Jeff Dimes. We all became good mates. The height of the entertainment was very small-sided football games over the 'Coronation Fields'. The difference between the other lads and me was that they all had elder brothers and sisters. Tony's brother Alan was much like us—a football fanatic; Jeff's brother was of the hippy type, and of course, Stan's sister was Pippa. I asked Stan if he liked his sister's music. He said it was all right. "She's still into Otis Redding at the moment. Her latest favourite is called 'Hard To Handle'. If you're thinking of buying that kind of music, Reg, try looking for a blue Stax label. That's what most of Pippa's are on. You won't find them in Woolworth's though. They have to be ordered from Rumbelows down the town."

Then Tony said, "Next week the old youth club is re-opening. If you fancy a squint, we can go and have a look."

The following Monday, the four of us strolled up to the youth club. On entering the club, I stared in amazement. Freshly painted walls, a bar, a football table, table tennis tables and a snooker table as well! But no mods and only one scooter outside! It belonged to a longhaired guy called Dave Brindle. It was a Lami (Lambretta).

In the corner of the club was a long skinny black box where two guys were playing records. Their names were Dave Collins, and an old school mate of mine, Brian Bannard. It was so different from the other record players that I'd seen. Two record decks side-by-side. Whilst one was playing, you set the other record up. The centre stem method of stacking eight at a time had now gone—it must have damaged the vinyl.

On looking around, I thought some of the teenagers were dead smart. Some were wearing small turn-ups on their Levis and button down collared checked shirts. Others were wearing light coloured trousers with a crease down the leg, which stayed dead sharp even after sitting down. The trousers were called 'Sta-Prest'.

The music was brilliant, a bit like Caribbean Soul with a distinctive beat. This new sound was called Reggae. The smart looking teenagers had different haircuts—nothing like the old mods. The guys had next to no hair at all and the girls had a light feathery cut. The new teenage cult was called skinheads. So, taken back by everything, Stan, Tony, Jeff and I immediately went to the club office and filled out the membership forms.

The next day, I had a meeting with my schoolteacher about job prospects. I was not very good at school. Instead of doing Maths and English, I spent most of my time in the woodwork room or repairing classmates' lockers.

Mr Calder, the woodwork teacher, said, "What would you like to be, son?"

"I'd like to be a boat builder," I said.

He said, "Most of that work is around the coast and when you get there, the boats will be made of glass fibre, and not wood. It will break your heart Reg."

"What about staying on?" I said.

"What?" he said. "You can't read or write properly; you have no chance of 'O' levels or 'A' levels. Get yourself a spirit level and go and earn yourself some money. St Albans College of Building for you (if they let you in). I'll write you a letter. On your way out, send the next boy in. You can leave today!"

So that was it. I got a job at a local sawmill, where they were willing to send me to college. I constructed 'made to measure' wooden suits—coffins to be exact. You might say a dead end job! Well, I suppose they were a little bit like boats. My starting wage was four shillings an hour, eight pounds a week. Overnight I was a millionaire, as most of the other school leavers were only on a fiver a week. And that's when it all started to happen, money in my pocket and soul music by the bucket load.

Whilst attending St. Albans College of Building, it didn't take them long to find out that I struggled to read and write. It was one day when I was sitting in a class of about twenty students. The teacher said, "Right lads, we've got a lot to get through. I'm going to read out the notes that I want you to store in your folders."

I was petrified! I knew that once again I would be the laughing stock of the class just like when I was at school. So instead of nipping to the toilet and disappearing, I half-heartedly raised my hand and tried to make a joke of the situation I was in.

When the teacher said, "Yes, Stickings, what's up?"

I replied, "I reckon you're 'aving a laugh Sir. I can't spell to save me life, getting me to write something down as you speak would be like trying to find out how many peas rabbits eat."

On that note the teacher just left the room and no one laughed at all. My mate Les Parker turned round from the desk in front of me and said, "Jesus Reg, you ain't 'arf in trouble mate. I reckon he's gone to get the Principal."

So there I was sitting at me desk, shitting myself, with "Nowhere To Run And Nowhere To Hide"—I reckon Martha Reeves And The Vandellas got the words just right in this song.

All of a sudden, the teacher and the Principal opened the class door and said, "Can you come outside for a moment, Stickings?"

Once the three of us were standing in the corridor, the Principal asked, "What's your problem Stickings?"

I said to the Principal, "I'm afraid I struggle to read and write and Mr Smith wanted us to write the words as he spoke. I feel that I'm wasting everybody's time. I think I should leave."

"Leave Stickings! You're going nowhere. Between you and me, you're one of the best carpenters we've got."

Instead of looking up and smiling at the Principal's comment, my head just bowed down to the floor and I could feel a tear trickling down my cheek.

At this point the Principal said, "What are you thinking about Stickings?"

"It seems like the big man upstairs either gives you a pair of hands to work with or a clever brain to write things."

"You're absolutely right Stickings and if you had both skills you would be lethal out there Son." He placed his hand on my shoulder and light-heartedly said, "Do you have any hobbies Reg?"

"I'm thinking of collecting records; I'm looking for 'choons' on the blue Stax label at the moment, Sir."

"Ah! Soul music eh! Leave it with me and I'll see what I've got at home."

Then he turned round to the teacher and said, "You see how easy it is to communicate with these young students. Try taking an interest in their hobbies. I think you should take your hat off to this young man for having the guts to let you know about his difficulties. Now, I want you to both work with each other and sort it out."

As we walked back into the class, I wiped my eyes quickly with the cuff of my sleeve. The teacher asked, "Who is the best writer in the class?"

Parker slings his hand up and says, "I'm by far the best writer in the class, Sir."

"Right then Parker, I want you to put these two pieces of carbon paper between your work and copy the notes for Stickings." He then said quietly, "Right then Reg, I want you to take this note to the lady downstairs on reception and we'll see what we can do."

So I went downstairs to see the receptionist. She read the note and asked if I did anything on Tuesday or Wednesday nights.

"Yes," I said, "Tuesday nights is Warners End youth club and Wednesdays is Bennetts End youth club, Why?"

"Well," she said, "you're going to have to miss one of them. We're sending you to the 'On the Move' English Group for people who struggle to read and write properly." After a quick phone call she said, "Right Mr Stickings, seven o'clock, Wednesday nights at Dacorum College in Hemel Hempstead. You should have just enough time to have your tea in between leaving the College of Building and going to your English lessons."

So that was it, no youth club for me on Wednesdays, I had to go to college. I hated going there at first but within a couple of weeks I got a bit too close for comfort with a married woman, for obvious reasons we'll call her Helen. She was a bit older than me but very sexy. It was after a couple of months when one night the teacher said, "I'm thinking of splitting you and Helen up."

"You can't do that miss; I teach Helen and she teaches me."

"It's what you're teaching each other that worries me. Get your hands above the table both of you."

"That's not fair miss; you've got to give us a chance."

"Okay," the teacher replied, "before you leave tonight I want you to start a sentence with the word 'Therefore'."

I rested my head in the palms of my hands and Helen asked, "What's up Reg?"

"I'm afraid that bitch of a teacher has got us. It's impossible to start a sentence with the word 'Therefore'. She's trying to make the rest of the class laugh at us like most of the other bloody teachers I've had."

Then Helen said excitedly, "Get your pen; I've got it."

I picked my pen up quickly and said, "Right, what is it you want me to write."

"There fore cows in a field."

I looked at Helen and said, "You silly twerp Helen! No wonder you're here. What a thing to say—you've got about as much intelligence as a pea!"

"So it looks like we're going to be split up Reg."

"Yes mate," I sighed "I'm afraid so."

Right at the end of the lesson the teacher tossed over a piece of chalk which I took out of the air with quite an impressive cricketer's catch. As I walked towards the blackboard I had no idea what I was going to write until I had written the word 'Therefore'. Then I proceeded with:

"Therefore is sometimes described by three dots—dot, dot, dot."

I lobbed the piece of chalk back to the teacher with a massive cheer from the rest of the class. Once Helen and I were outside of the class, I said goodbye to her as I knew deep inside that I would not be returning. At that point I knew that I was going to have to get through life on just wit alone and nothing else.

Back at the youth club, I met another skinhead called Clive Bartlett, whose brother Terry was an old mod. We were round at Clive's house one day, when Terry said, "Do you wanna see my record collection, Reg?"

"Not 'alf," I said.

I was expecting to see a small record box like Auntie Carol's, but was I in for a surprise! In Terry's room there was a chest of drawers with a record player on the top. The top drawer had two handles on the front. With both hands, Terry carefully opened the drawer. I was speechless. The whole drawer was dedicated to records, which were lying flat rather than upright (not the best way to store them, but good enough in this case). It was all the different labels that took my breath away. Looking down the right hand side was the Blue Beat collection—not one or two, but at least twenty to thirty... Then there was the light blue Stax pile, then the black English Tamla Motown, then the orange and blue Trojan. There were about ten separate piles and so neatly stacked. The Hot Wax multicoloured label, the Motown imports, and then the yellow and brown Tamla pile.

What a wonderful sight, let alone what they sounded like! And when Terry started to play them, I wasn't disappointed. For at least six hours it was an education at its best.

What impressed me most was the way Terry handled them. He carefully removed the record from its sleeve, a quick wipe with an 'Emitex' record cleaning cloth, then he placed it on the record deck as if it were bone china. On the side of the record player was a lever that slowly lowered the stylus down onto the record and when the sound kicked in... well, every one was a gem!

Terry's words were, "feel the beat of this one... listen to the lyrics of this one... wait for the trumpets... can you hear the sax? ... wait for the

New Orleans guitar..." and so it went on. It wasn't until it was time to leave this heavenly place that I realised my search for soul had begun.

When I got home, I emptied the top drawer of my own chest of drawers, lined the bottom with some larder paper and placed my copy of "Don't Sleep In The Subway" in the top corner. I had no idea that this record was going to be the first of thousands.

Chapter 3

The Youth Club Years

It seemed that new releases were coming out every week. The favourites at the youth club were:

Tears Of A Clown	Smokey Robinson
Elizabethan Reggae	Boris Gardner
Wet Dream	Max Romeo
Jimmy Mack	Martha Reeves & The Vandellas
If I Had A Hammer	Nicky Thomas
Blowin' In The Wind	Stevie Wonder
Let Your Yeah Be Yeah	The Pioneers
You Keep Me Hanging On	Supremes
Give Me Just A Little More Time	Chairman Of The Board
Black Pearl	Horace Faith
Montego Bay	Freddie Note And The Rudies
Young Gifted And Black	Bob And Marcia
You Can Get It If You Really Want	Desmond Decker
What Greater Love	Teddy Brown

And so on….

Most of these tracks you could buy from Rumbelows, a domestic appliance shop. The Motown tracks were on the British release black Motown label. Reggae was on the Trojan label—orange and blue or just orange. It was getting the more obscure tracks that was the problem, as I knew the sounds I wanted but had no idea where to buy them.

One of the records that I had trouble with was 'Tribute To A King' by William Bell on a blue Stax. I own it now, but it took a long time to find. It's a tribute to the great Otis Redding by one of his old friends—a good record to own if you are a soul fan.

Most of the older soul records on Stax or Atlantic that I owned were given to me by some of the older lads in our area, or I found them at the church jumble sale. With most of my wages going on the latest Reggae or Tamla Motown releases, hard to find tunes had to take a back seat for a while. I didn't mind as the top drawer that I dedicated to records was gradually filling up with the new releases.

Also in the early days of collecting records three or four white singers found their way into the record drawer along with Petula Clark. Records such as 'Knocking On Heaven's Door' by Bob Dylan, 'Sometimes' by Mireille Mathieu, and one of my all-time favourites, 'Something In The Air' by Thunderclap Newman. Then the sound of 'This Boy' by The Beatles taught me that sometimes the B sides of records are better than the A sides.

Going to the youth club was a good way to communicate with friends of the same interest—clothes, records and football. We all learned from each other, it appeared that the local council was spending on all of the youth clubs in our area. 'Square One' in Adeyfield and Gadebridge Youth Club were refurbished at the same time as Bennetts End. Then Warners End Youth Club a little after and because they were open on different nights, you had something to do every night of the week.

I personally thought the lads at Adeyfield's Square One looked the smartest, because the majority were a couple of years older than the Bennetts End crew. They wore mohair suits, smart strides and hand-made shoes. They seemed to be slightly in front, fashion wise. Especially two lads I admired, John Bell and Biddy Baxter. In my opinion, if they were wearing it, everyone would be following suit in a couple of months' time. The older boys wore suits because they were old enough to get into the nightclubs, but we had a couple of years to go, especially me being so small. Even buying the right clothes was a challenge. As I was earning a decent wage (at least £3 per week more than most of my mates) I decided that I could afford to use some money on train fares. So I started travelling into London, which gave me access to the latest fashionable clothing. At first I stuck to just Oxford Street. My favourite shops were Take Six, Guys & Dolls, Lord John's, Ravels and the Squire shop. It was not long before I had at least a dozen button-down collared shirts, Brutus, Ben Sherman, Jaytex etc, a couple of Fred Perrys and a pair of Sta-Prest. I even bought a Trilby just to look the part.

One day, I decided to walk back from Oxford Street to Euston. I cut down a back alley called Hanway Street to eventually get to Tottenham Court Road when I heard that old Box Tops number 'The Letter'. The sound was coming from an open window above an open front door, with an old winding wooden staircase inside. Looking up at the open window, it seemed to be quite busy up there, but dare I go in or not?

The next record kicked in. It was 'The Pied Piper' by Bob & Marcia. Both records I wanted dearly. I had to go in, but before I did, I separated my money into different pockets, just in case… I walked up the rickety stairs. At the top was an old wooden door, with a round handled tin rim lock on it. By then another record was playing—'Free The People' by Winston Groovy, another gem.

I opened the door at the top of the stairs and walked straight in. Talk about spot the white guy! There were about six black "zoot" type geezers this side of the counter and a massive bloke on the other side, and the room was only about 10 foot square.

"And what can we do for you, little whitey?" said the big guy.

"I'm interested in some of your records. Are they expensive?" I said nervously.

One of the lads this side of the counter said, looking down at the bag I was holding.

"If you can afford to shop at Take Six, you can afford to buy records from here. What have you bought?"

"An ice blue Fred Perry with a red and black trimming," I said, "but it won't fit any of you lot, it's the smallest they make."

This seemed to break the ice. The chap behind the counter laughed and said, "What you after then, Chalkie?"

"The last three that you've played," I replied.

He got the Bob & Marcia and the Winston Groovy from a new cardboard box on the counter. But he had to look for the Box Tops number on one of the shelves that went all around the room. I had never seen so many pieces of vinyl in my life.

The chap behind the counter said, "Write your name and address on this list, and I will send you a monthly catalogue," which I did.

When I left the shop, I kept looking behind me, but everything seemed to be all right. Then when I got to Tottenham Court Road, I realised this was the place to buy record players. The shops were full of them. And because there were so many shops, I reckon you would definitely be able to strike a bargain along this road. Whilst walking to Euston, I was desperately trying to remember the record titles I wanted.

Especially now I had found the right place to buy them—what a find...

Chapter 4

From Youth Clubs To Night Clubs

On my way home from work one day, I saw Stan Brewster hiding in our side alley.

"All right Stan? What are you doing?" I said.

"I'm hiding from the new kid at our school. He's mad; comes from Manchester. He's been casing me for two hours—I haven't been home yet. He's like a big grizzly bear!"

I thought Stan was off his rocker… "Come round my house and have some tea. He won't be around now."

Oh, how wrong I was! As we came out the alley, there was a massive roar.

"It's him," said Stan, "Run!!"

We ran into my house petrified and locked the doors. After a few minutes, we started laughing our heads off. "He's like a big Yogi Bear! His name is Paul Bohknecht. A Mancunian, with a dad from Germany, but worst of all is his football club!"

I said, "You haven't been winding him up have you Stan?"

"I don't have to Reg, he supports City!" said Stan, a staunch Man United fan.

From that day on, Paul Bohknecht's name was to change. After a few weeks, Stan said, "That new kid at school's a great bloke. I've asked him to come up the youth club, but don't call him Paul. Me and Jeff Dimes call him Yogi,"

"He won't beat me up will he Stan?"

"Not as long as you call him Yogi, you'll be all right."

So that was it; Yogi became part of our little crew. A couple of weeks later, Yogi invited Stan and me round his house. So as not to cramp his parents' style, we sat in his mother's kitchen. Yogi brought a small record player down from upstairs and some of his records. His records were unique—a man after our own hearts.

In my opinion, the best record Yogi played that night was a Reggae sound called 'The Law Part II' by Andy Capp on a blue and white Duke label. The three of us started to play records about 7 o'clock and finished about quarter to one. As Stan and I began to walk home, we spoke about Yogi's brilliant records. Stan said, "Yogi's asked me to go out to a night club on Monday, so I'm not going up the youth club. Why don't you come with us?"

"If you don't think he'd mind, I'd love to," I said.

"You'll be all right Reg, we'll just have to dress up a bit smarter than we do up the youth club, won't we?"

On the following Monday, I polished up my Doctor Martens and I got Mum to iron my Sta-Prest and one of my Sherman's. As I didn't have a jacket, I wore my Brutus tank top. I thought I looked all right, until I got to Yogi's house, then I realised I was completely wrong.

When Yogi opened his front door, his words were, "There's no way he's going like that! You don't go to a night club in a tank top and DMs!"

He was adamant that I wouldn't get in. I had to agree that if I didn't, I was on my own. So off we went to the Civic Hall in St. Albans.

It wasn't just the footwear that might cause a problem but my height. We got to the entrance and met Jeff Dimes and John Lee. I stood between the four others and we walked straight into the ballroom, without being seen by the bouncers.

Inside, it was breathtaking. Top people, top music and top dance floor; and on this dance floor we learned our first dance steps. We didn't move a lot; it was a bit like a Reggae shuffle, standing on the spot, all in a line. The worst dancer at the time was Stan Brewster. All these years later, he still is!

It was the year of 1971. In my opinion, the public had been ripped off big time by decimalisation. The thru'penny Milky Way was now two and a half new pence, (sixpence in old money) and the Mars Bar was now 5 new pence (an old shilling), twice as much as before! It seemed that everything you bought was twice the old price. This was also the year my beloved Liverpool FC got to the FA Cup Final against Arsenal and the colour television had just been invented. My dad was the first person in the street to rent a new colour telly—I had asked him because Liverpool was in the final. But guess what? One week before kick-off I managed to get a ticket! I was on £15 a week and my one-pound ticket cost me a tenner. I know Liverpool lost—Charlie George hit the winner—but this was still the best 'tenner' I'd ever spent. You never forget your first cup final.

Soon after, I had to go shopping in London. I bought a pair of real leather Kingsway Loafers and a bronze and blue tonic mohair suit. Looking back to the day I went to buy that tonic suit, I felt that I had rehearsed a part in the Julia Roberts' film *Pretty Woman* in real life.

The Number One shop to buy two-tone tonic strides was Davis's of Tottenham High Road. I strolled in and asked the shop assistant if I could see the tonic mohair trousers. As I browsed around, I actually overheard the shop assistant say to his governor, "I've got another little kid wanting to look at the tonic stand".

The governor said, "Tell him we're shutting for lunch and stocktaking."

As I walked out of the shop I felt like shit, especially after travelling all the way from Hemel by train. I strolled down the road a bit and came across a small tailor's shop where a Jewish chap was operating a sewing machine. The thing that brought my attention to this small shop was that the tailors ran a Sketchleys' dry cleaning service. I poked my head in the door and asked the Jewish gentleman if he sold tonics.

His reply was, "Have I got something for you son! Come in and try this jacket on."

Well, it looked absolutely perfect. I said it was tonic strides I was interested in, not a jacket.

"I know, but this is a suit and the jacket looks as if it was made for you. Here put the trousers on, you're a 24-inch waist aren't you?"

I put the strides on and after the man had tucked up the bottoms, I looked the dog's bollocks. I moved my leg slightly, just to see the suit change colour from bronze to blue. I asked the chap if I wanted an inch turn-up just sitting on top of my loafer shoe, how long will it take?

The chap replied, "The time it takes you to nip over the road to the Wimpy bar and have a burger."

"Come on then," I said, "hit me with the price."

"It's not cheap son, I'll do the alterations for nothing, but I'm afraid the price of the suit is 12 pounds 50 pence."

I thought to myself, "Oh shit! Nearly a week's wages. But I've got to have it."

"OK," I said, "on one condition. When it's finished, can you put it in one of your plastic Sketchley's cleaning bags and supply me with a coat hanger as I'm travelling by train and I don't want to get it dirty."

"Of course I can. Now go and have your Wimpy and I'll see you in about 20 minutes."

True to his word, 20 minutes later and a smear of tomato sauce on the side of my mouth, the suit was ready. As I was walking down the road with my new suit hanging over my shoulder, changing colour with every step, I strolled into Davis's and asked the assistant and his governor if they sold socks. Guess what? I didn't feel like shit any more.

The new suit was a must, as at the age of 17, we were graduating from youth clubs to the nightclubs and I did not want to be dodging bouncers wearing Doctor Martens (or upsetting Yogi again). The records we were dancing to around this time were Reggae or Tamla Motown. We bought everything produced by Prince Buster, 'Moon River' by Greyhound, 'Double Barrel' by Dave and Ansell Collins and all the latest Motown hits. The Philly sound; Billy Paul, O'Jays, Intruders etc were now reaching our record collection. Also, I bought an LP by Bobby Womack just for one track called 'Harry Hippy', but after listening to all the other tunes, *Understanding* by Bobby Womack became my best LP of all time, as did the artist—of all the soul singers I have listened to, Bobby is my favourite.

My best mate at the time was Stan Brewster, but Stan was not the person I was going to spend the rest of my life searching for soul with. It was going to be Yogi. Stan was more of a Reggae fan than Yogi and me. Stan was getting rare Reggae sounds by ordering them from abroad, whilst Yogi and I were collecting the more soulful tunes. So the three of us were still well into our music, mad about football and had a good eye for fashion (so we thought!).

Stan had started working by now and managed to get a job in St Albans at an insurance company, which came in handy, as I was at St Albans College of Building so we could travel to work together. He always made me late, spiking his hair up like Rod Stewart. Then we would meet up at lunchtimes. These were spent buying records and planning the weekends. House parties, shopping in London, football matches etc—there was never a dull moment.

When going in to London shopping or looking for records, it was a lot more comfortable with mates rather than on your own. We would venture down a lot more side streets. One day we ended up in Soho market and found a stall holder selling vinyl records, which were a lot cheaper than Contempo Records shop in Hanway Street, but you did have to check them for scratches, cracks or warping. Some good sounds were found in Soho, there were also a lot of record shops around this area right next door to some seedy places that Soho is more famous for.

A few weeks later my brother Geoff and I had saved some money up and decided to buy a new stereo record player. The only problem was we knew 'naff all' about buying stereos. So we decided the only way we could make the right choice was to buy it by ear. I took my copy of 'Shaft' by Issac Hayes to London with us.

The larger stereo shops in London's Tottenham Court Road had demonstration rooms, normally downstairs. We deliberately dressed down a bit as we were carrying so much money. We were wearing our Levi jackets and jeans. Stuffed in our Levi jacket pockets we had £200 in cash. Nowadays we are talking about the equivalent of £1,500—an awful lot of money to be carried by two teenagers.

When we walked into one of the shops, a chap asked, "Can I help you two?"

"Yes," we said, "We would like to buy a stereo."

I thought we were going to get the same reaction as when I bought my first tonic mohair suit.

The shop assistant said to his governor, "I've got two kids here wanting to buy a stereo. What shall I do?"

The shop assistant's boss said, "Do you want to buy a stereo, lads?"

I quickly said, "Yes please, but we want to buy it by ear, I've bought one of my own records with me."

The big boss said, "Take these lads downstairs, but don't let them touch anything." Then he said, "Stereos don't come cheap lads, but we do have HP agreements as long as you have references."

When we got downstairs, there were all kinds of record decks, speakers, amps, tuners and tape recorders. My brother and I were amazed but didn't want to show it. Then the chap played a record, it sounded all right but it was a Mario Lanza type sound. This was no good to us—we hated that type of music.

"Can you play our record, mate?"

The chap seemed to know what he was at, as he wiped my copy of 'Shaft' with an Emitex record cleaning cloth.

As it started to play, I said to Geoff, "What do you think?"

He said quietly, "It seems a bit tinny."

"It seems a bit tinny, mate," I said.

Geoff then said, "What's the best speakers you've got?"

"That would be Celestion speakers. They're not cheap but they are the best we've got. They have solid teak boxes."

"Stick 'em on then," Geoff said, "we'll give 'em a whirl."

It was amazing! The best we'd ever heard Issac Hayes—sounds we hadn't heard before on our little record player—violins, drums, cymbals and guitars—you could hear the lot.

"Okay mate, so what've we got then."

"Pioneer Belt Driven Deck, Zalua Amp, Celestion top of the range speakers."

"That's great mate, so how much then?"

The shop assistant said, "I will check with the governor. It adds up to £185."

"Sounds good," we said, "let's go and see him."

When we got upstairs, the assistant showed the list of items to the boss and he started tapping out an HP agreement. "I am afraid that it's going to be, with a £25 deposit, the sum of £3.26 per week for 52 weeks.

"What about cash?" we said.

"If you could raise that sum of money together, I will do it for £175 cash."

I undid the button of my Levi jacket breast pocket and coolly laid £100 in tenners on the counter. Then Geoff did the same and counted out £75. Whilst waving the money in front of their eyes, Geoff said "What about those Keff headphones, and a spare needle."

The assistant and his governor seemed a bit gob-smacked that we had the money in our pockets. The boss said, "OK, I will give you the stylus and instead of £20 for the headphones you can have them for £15."

And so the deal was struck.

Geoff said, "I want it all boxed up ready for next Saturday as we'll be stopping on a yellow line in me Dad's car."

Geoff and I left the shop quite pleased with ourselves...

Chapter 5

A Special Night Out With Me Dad

Two very special things happened to me whilst travelling between Hemel Hempstead and Liverpool.

One was finding a magazine, which you will all hear about later in the book, and the other was to do with my beloved Liverpool Football Club. It was a case of being in the right place at the right time, or as I am always preaching to my son Jack and daughter Holly, "you get out of life what you put in" and on this occasion if you were a Liverpool fan the event I was about to witness was way beyond comprehension.

I was travelling back from Anfield, keeping a low profile, whilst browsing through my freshly printed *Liverpool Evening Echo*. This situation was nothing new as I was only following my dad's advice. I listened when he was trying to educate me on 'street cred'.

Now and then he would say, "I don't mind you travelling all that way to Liverpool but you're only a little lad. I want you to be aware—there's a lot of queer folk and troublemakers out there. Keep yourself to yourself and you should be all right."

Now, as I was saying, I was travelling back from Anfield, (not the happiest of bunnies—a one-all draw with Coventry at home was simply not good enough). I was feeling a little down in the dumps when some geezer approached me.

His words were, "Who do you support then?"

I thought to myself, "here we go," and replied quietly, "I'm a Liverpool fan."

"You reckon?" replied the bloke. "How many games have you seen this season then?"

"About twenty," I replied.

"That's every game so far, isn't it?"

"No, I missed the one against Spurs; it was an evening game and I couldn't get there."

"Where do you live?" he asked I thought this was getting a bit to close to comfort.

"Watford," I replied.

"Well I'm impressed," said the bloke, "I've been told to give these tickets to London-based Liverpool fans and I think you deserve a couple. They're for a small do at Thames studios next Wednesday, right by Euston Station." As the chap disappeared into the next carriage, I placed the two tickets in my Levi jacket breast pocket.

Every Saturday, when Liverpool was playing at Anfield, I'd always get home just in time for *Match of the Day*. I'd walk in my front door and Dad would say, "Mum's makin' yer some toast, Liverpool are on the telly in a minute, did yer get a program and the *Echo*?"

As I handed the requested items to me Dad and sat down beside him I said, "Some geezer come up to me on the train, Dad."

For a couple of seconds, Dad took his eyes off the new colour telly and replied, "What did he want? Did he look like a queer?"

"Not really, Dad. He asked me how many games I'd seen, then he gave me a couple of tickets for Thames Studios next Wednesday."

I passed the tickets to my dad. After a small pause, he said, "It's not that far Son. You've got nothing to lose, but you're not going on yer own. I'll come with yer."

The following Wednesday, we left our house for Thames Studios straight after our tea. When we arrived there was no activity whatsoever. I tried the main door and peered through the darkened window, then said to my dad, "It's all shut, Dad, there's nothing on here."

"Well we're a bit early Son, let's wait and see."

At that moment, a giant of a man peered through the same window, then I must have caught his eye, as he said, "I know you; I've seen you before in the Kop at Anfield."

I started thinking to myself, "Yeah, all right mate, we're talking over 45,000 Liverpool fans, I'm only three foot high and you reckon you know who I am?"

Then this man, called Fred I found out later, said, "Looking in the Kop from the penalty spot, right hand side of the goalpost, right at the front of the second tier where the little path is which runs straight through the middle of the terraces. That's where you stand!"

To my astonishment, Fred described my spot on the Kop to perfection.

Then he said, "Haven't you got that elongated banner with the words Liverpool F.C. running through the small part of the Union Jack?"

"Yes," I replied, "That's me" (and guess what guys, all these years later I've still got the same banner in a drawer by my bed).

Fred then asked, "What's the spec like where you stand? Do you have to stand on anything to see?"

I gave Fred a quick wink and said, "I sometimes stand on an old tin can to gain height, Fred."

What my dad didn't know was that the old tin can I was standing on was a Party Seven full of beer for me and my mates to drink. I knew Fred had a good idea what I was going on about. Then I said, "The other reason I stand where I do is because when I feel the movement in the crowd, if I duck quick enough under the barrier I can get a bit of breathing space standing on the little path whilst looking for my now slightly beaten up old tin can."

Fred said, "Have you got tickets for tonight lads?"

"Yes," I said, "What's it all about?"

"Well," said Fred, "The last time I was given tickets for something like this was when Alan Rudkin the Liverpool boxer was on the *This Is Your Life* program. What the producers of the program wanted was a London-based audience with a Liverpool connection. Tonight we think it's Cilla."

"You don't mean Cilla Black do yer?"

"Oh don't worry, they're bloody good nights whoever it is. Come with me, we're all in the pub next door."

Then my dad piped up with, "What about the boy?"

Fred said, "He'll be alright, we'll stick him in the corner somewhere."

At this point, it was obvious to me that Dad had no idea about my other life, being a young boozy Liverpool fan. Whilst walking to the alehouse, Fred whispered to me, "When we're in the pub I'll have to buy you a soft drink."

I replied, "That's alright mate."

As soon as we entered the pub, Dad and I sat at a small table in the corner while Fred bought the drinks. It was when Fred was carrying the drinks back to the table where we were sitting I realised something amazing was about to happen. I looked at Fred's face and he was white as a ghost with an element of excitement in his eyes.

As he went to sit down his words were, "It's not Cilla lads, Joe Mercer and Tommy Docherty are sitting in the other bar."

"Oh my God!" I replied, "It can't be Keegan or Toshack can it? I know they're both brilliant but they're far too young for *This Is Your Life*. What if it's Roger Hunt or Cally?" (Ian Callaghan).

Within a few minutes, a frenzy was stirring around this small pub, then when we all finally got seated in the studio a pair of curtains parted, revealing a cinema screen. The lights dimmed and Eamonn Andrews appeared on the screen with his big red book, hiding behind a brick column as the Liverpool Express pulled into Euston station. Then when the train pulled up and stopped, the doors opened and out walked the Liverpool team.

Eamonn Andrews made a dash towards them and said those immortal words: "Manager of Liverpool Football Club, tonight, Bill Shankley 'This Is Your Life'."

Even now, as I am writing this, the tears are welling up behind my glasses. What an accolade to feel I was a part of this man's life! Just imagine a small television studio filled with the most famous football stars. There was Alf Ramsey, Tommy Docherty, Jock Stein, Sir Matt Busby, Joe Mercer, Geoff Hurst, Bertie Mee, at least three Liverpool teams old and new, me and 'me dad', Bob Paisley, the Scottish international squad and countless other people connected with the football world. Nessie, Bill Shankley's wife, seemed so proud as she stood beside him (he thought she was sitting at home back in Liverpool).

This was a very special night out with 'me dad'. It's just as I said, in most cases you get out of life what you put in and in this case, that's exactly what happened.

REGGIE'S CHOICE:
FAVOURITES FROM THE CALI

Tribute To A King	William Bell
What Becomes Of The Broken Hearted?	Jimmy Ruffin
Harry Hippy	Bobby Womack
Keep On Trucking	Eddie Kendricks
Brown Baby	Billy Paul
Back Stabbers	O'Jays
Stoned Love	Diana Ross
Sex Machine	James Brown
Just My Imagination	The Temptations
Private Number	William Bell & Judy Clay
Shaft	Issac Hayes
Walk In The Night	Junior Walker
Feel The Need	Detroit Emeralds
SOS	Edwin Starr
Brothers Gonna Work It Out	Willy Hutch
Love Theme	Barry White
Sittin' On The Dock Of The Bay	Otis Redding
Standing In The Shadows Of Love	Four Tops
Where Did Our Love Go?	Donny Elbert
Why Can't We Live Together?	Timmy Thomas
Love Train	O'Jays
Mister Magic Man	Wilson Pickett
Pillow Talk	Sylvia
Theme From The Men	Issac Hayes

Chapter 6

California Ballroom (The Cali)

Once I had a taste of the nightclub scene and managed to purchase the right clothing—shoes, jacket, suit etc, it did not take me long to venture out into other nightspots. I managed to get into a club which had just opened in Hemel town centre. The club was called Stripes. Once inside, I was astonished; the dance floor was very small with sunken areas and raised platforms. It was a seedy place, similar to the Moloko Plus bar in the film *Clockwork Orange*, and when I went to buy a drink at the bar, I was gob-smacked! Right before my eyes was Pippa Brewster, serving drinks in the Stripes uniform. The uniform included green Lurex hot pants! What had they done to the lovely looking modette I once knew?

I looked around a few different nightclubs such as the New Penny and the Top Rank in Watford, then the Mecca in Stevenage, but nothing could compare to the California Ballroom in Dunstable. At 'The Cali' the management booked really class acts such as Stevie Wonder in his early days, Jimmy Ruffin, Martha Reeves and the Vandellas and most of the Philadelphia artists—the O'Jays, Billy Paul, Harold Melvin and the Blue Notes. I also saw the Platters, Drifters, Edwin Starr and many, many more.

In the late sixties, early seventies the Cali was the place to be. There were three bars for the main dance floor and one downstairs with a small dance floor called the Devil's Den, which was situated by the cloakroom. The Cali set-up was completely right because every bar was nowhere near the magnificent dance floor. They were all situated in small rooms of their own.

If I can remember rightly, the dance floor was about quarter of the size of a football pitch. It was huge and there was always a fantastic atmosphere. The dance floor was made of real wood and there was a massive mirror ball hanging from the centre of the roof.

The Cali was the best real ballroom I had ever been to. Five hours on a Saturday night listening to someone like Jimmy Ruffin, with a young lady in tow, was my idea of paradise. This is what we worked darned hard for all week—those five hours.

In the early stages of going to the Cali, I went with friends called Clive Bartlett, Jeff Dimes, my brother Geoff and some of the Adeyfield lads; Biddy Baxter, John Bell, Keith Leech etc. But as time went on, say late '71-'72, I met up with Yogi again. He had a little crew who loved the music as much as I did, so I started going clubbing with them. There were five of us altogether, Yogi, Phil Makepeace, Dave Creasey, me and a little Fijian lad called Tejeshua dat Ram, we called him TD for short.

Along with going to the Cali, we started to hit many of the London concert halls, Hammersmith Odeon, the Rainbow Finsbury Park, London Palladium, Camden Roundhouse or anywhere that classy soul acts were playing. We even went to the Gaumont Theatre one night, in Ipswich where the Stylistics and Jimmy Ruffin were playing. The round trip for this concert alone was around 240 miles. So you see travelling a few miles was not a problem. If we knew where our music was at, that's where we went.

On a Friday night, our clothes were all laid out ready waiting for that exclusive phone call from Yogi or me.

The phone call would go something like:

"Pack your bag, we're going to 'Caister' for the weekend":

"We'll be around at 8 o'clock. Wear something casual, we're going to a concert."

"Put on your strides; we are going clubbing."

"We're only going to the Cali tonight but tomorrow after the football we're out at a concert."

And so it went on...

We always had something to do and most of the time all five of us were up for it, whatever it was.

One Friday night at the Cali we met up with the Redbourn girls; their little crew consisted of Rose, Sue, Trudy, Denise and a couple of friends that used to tag along with them. Redbourn is a small village between Dunstable and Hemel. On Sundays, if it was a weekend when the boys were local, we would go round for the Redbourn girls and make a day of it. If we were all packed in one car, the cassette player went on and we would all start singing. Sometimes the boys were Marvin Gaye and the girls were Diana Ross, or William Bell and Judy Clay or we were all Gladys Knight and the Pips and so on.

Every moment possible we were surrounded by music and we all loved every minute. Entertaining ourselves and listening to that sweet soul music was what our lives were all about. We thought we were soul connoisseurs; we probably were in the area that we lived, but as this kind of music is so vast and there are so many different types of soul sounds it would be impossible to own them all. The records I am listing through the book are my own personal choice at that time and place.

We had no idea what was going down in the underground clubs up north (such as the Twisted Wheel and the Golden Torch). The five of us were happy with the sounds we were hearing at the Cali. Yogi and I had Torch membership cards but by the time we got round to using them, it was too late and the Torch was shut down. Our biggest regret was not going when Major Lance was playing live. We both had the 'live' LP but that was as close as we got.

We loved the Cali and that was it! We had some fantastic nights there and still rate the place as one of the top venues we had the privilege of going to.

Chapter 7

Hovering In A Three Foot Circle

In early '73, the music started changing. Funkier sounds started to take over at the Cali. Although I liked some of the James Brown type music such as 'It's A Man's World', 'King Heroin' and 'Hey America', I found the funkier sounds at the time were a bit too heavy for me and I was getting disillusioned by it all. I preferred the more soulful tunes with violins and a little Motown type beat in the background. 'Love Train' by the O'Jays was a favourite of mine along with everything else from Philadelphia.

In the February of 1973, I was travelling back on a train from watching Liverpool FC when I picked up a magazine left on a spare seat. I could not believe it. It was a *Blues & Soul* magazine and Billy Paul, a favourite of mine, was on the front cover. Who would leave a magazine of this quality behind? What a find it turned out to be—it's as if it were meant. I browsed through the pages. There was a questionnaire page, which had been answered by a hippy-type Hendrix fan, because most of the questions were filled in like this:

Favourite Artist	Jimi Hendrix
Favourite R&B Group	Jimi Hendrix Experience
Favourite R&B Producers	Jimi Hendrix

And so it went on.

The *Blues & Soul* magazine was No. 102, February 2nd 1973, and at the time, the Top Ten British Soul Singles were:

1. Love Train (CBS1181)	O'Jays
2. Why Can't We Live Together (MOJO 2027.012)	Timmy Thomas
3. Feel The Need (JANUS 6146.020)	Detroit Emeralds
4. Superfly (BUDDAH 2011.156)	Curtis Mayfield
5. Killing Me Softly (ATLANTIC 10282)	Roberta Flack
6. Gonna Make You An Offer You Can't Refuse (BUG 27)	Jimmy Helms
7. Harry Hippy (UA 35456)	Bobby Womack
8. The Look Of Love (MOTOWN 844)	Gladys Knight & The Pips
9. We Did It (LONDON 10403)	Sly Johnson
10. Harlem Shuffle (CONTEMPO 4)	Bob & Earl

This magazine was such good reading, the following week, when I went around Bennetts End shops to pick up my *Jimmy Hill Football Weekly*, I placed a standing order for the *Blues & Soul* as well. This new magazine led the lads and me on an even stranger journey. Searching for Soul!!!

In the summer of 1973, the lads and I found that we weren't going to our beloved Cali on a regular basis. The heavier funky sounds that were mainly played downstairs in the Devil's Den were now being played upstairs in the main Cali ballroom (not our cup of tea really). We were only going to the Cali when the artists we liked were playing such as Edwin Starr, Junior Walker or when some of the Philadelphia groups were performing. If it was a disco night we knew the tunes we loved would be very few and far between our Cali days were coming to an end. More and more we were going away at the weekends!

The Bali Hi was still a favourite down in Margate and when we were in Kent we would always visit my cousins and reminisce our teenage days staying at my Auntie and Uncle's house. Other weekends we would go to Manchester and stay at Yogi's Nan's house. Yogi's Nan lived in an area called Hulme. To me it appeared quite a rough place to live, not a place to walk alone on your own, especially being a person from the South. But as Yogi used to be a local, he knew where to walk and when to keep your mouth shut.

Living with Yogi's Nan was his Uncle John. When we arrived on a Friday night, Yogi's Uncle John would insist that we went to his Buffalo Lodge with him. Uncle John's mates loved us! It would be a laugh from start to finish especially when we tried swapping accents. John's mates would try talking with a London accent and we would be the Mancunians. They always looked forward to seeing us as much as we did them.

On the Saturday, we would go shopping for records and clothes and if Yogi's team Man City was playing at home, we went to the match. Saturday nights, Yogi would take us to the big nightclubs where the City and United footballers would sometimes go. Players like Colin Bell or maybe Mike Summerbee, 'Bestie' or Dennis Law etc.

The nightclubs were called Rafters, Jilly's and Cloisters. If I can remember rightly they were situated in Oxford Street in Manchester. The music was more a disco type sound, easy to come by records that were in the record charts and the audience were all out for a good time— whatever music was playing they didn't seem to mind. The clubs were all dead smart, well decorated with posh furnishings. Also they had the latest flashing disco lighting. It was a bit nervy when we went in these clubs because we were Southerners right in the heart of Manchester. We had to be aware of our London accents, keeping a low profile and letting Yogi do most of the talking. I always wore long-sleeved shirts as I had a Liverpool Football Club tattoo on my arm and I don't think this would have gone down well with any Man U fans bearing a grudge. Liverpool was winning quite a few trophies for a change and the Man U fans didn't like it. Also I would have been petrified if United or City had played a London football club on the days we were clubbing in Manchester.

On the way home from a Manchester weekender Yogi said, "How 'ya feeling Reg?"

"A little bit knackered but not too bad." I said. "Why's that?"

"You know we sent for those international soul club membership cards? Well they arrived last week and there is one on tonight at the Top Rank in Watford and Al Green is on."

"You must be joking!" I said. "Of course I'm up for it. You kept that quiet, what time do you want me ready?"

"I'll be around at 8 o'clock." Yogi said, so off we went.

When we got inside the Top Rank, there was a few already in but not the amount of people I was expecting for such a brilliant artist of Al Green's quality—and was he quality? One of the best I had ever seen. I put Al Green on the same pedestal as my all time favourites Bobby Womack and Marvin Gaye. Every song was sung perfectly. It was not just his all time best sellers 'Let's Stay Together' and 'Tired Of Being Alone' but all the other songs were brilliant as well; 'Call Me'; 'Sha La La (Make Me Happy)'; 'Look What You Done For Me' and 'How Can You Mend A Broken Heart?'

The list was endless and sung with such commitment, with a voice you could die for. What an end to a perfect weekend.

When Al Green had finished, the DJ played the night out with some top soul dance tunes: 'Step By Step' by Joe Simon; 'Love On A Mountain Top' by Robert Knight' and 'Sweetest Feeling' by Jackie Wilson.

Whilst the DJ was playing Love Train by the O'Jays, Yogi said, "Have you clocked the two fellas at the back of the room, Reg?"

When I saw them, I could not help it, I had to stop dancing and just watch with disbelief, I had never seen dancing like it, they sort of 'Hovered Within A Three Foot Circle' with one arm behind their back and the other at a right angle with a clenched fist. On the hand with the clenched fist, they were each wearing a black leather glove.

I said to Yogi, "Look at the hand with the black leather glove, they appear to be imitating the logo on our membership cards."

I looked at what they were wearing; their strides were like a black parallel Sta-Prest and they wore a black skin-tight short sleeve shirt with a small collar and breast pockets. On one of the breast pockets a round black and white patch type badge was sewn and they wore a black sports wristband.

Yogi said, "I'll dance a bit closer and see what's on the badge."

After a few seconds he said, "It says the Torch, Stoke on Trent. That's the place we should have gone to last year when Major Lance was playing live. We'll have to look into this—I've never seen dancing like it, and so in time with the music too."

On the way home I said to Yogi, "I felt a bit uncomfortable dancing on the Mancunians' patch in the club you took me to on Saturday, but the two Stoke boys seemed quite happy tonight at the Rank."

Yogi said, "Well they were there for the same reason as us. It's the music."

I was absolutely knackered when I got home after such a brilliant weekend. Whilst lying in bed, I stuck the Keff Cans on my head and listened to my *Best Of Al Green* album, but I could not help thinking about the way the two Stoke lads moved on the dance floor.

REGGIE'S CHOICE:
FIRST TASTE OF DANCE SOUL BEFORE WIGAN

Sweetest Feeling	Jackie Wilson
Love Train	O'Jays
Sliced Tomatoes	Just Brothers
Honey Bee	Johnny Johnson
Feel The Need In Me	Detroit Emeralds
I Had It All The Time	Tyrone Davis
Baby Hit And Run	Contours
A Man Like Me	Jimmy James
Hawaii Five 0	The Ventures
Apples, Peaches, Pumpkin Pie	Jay & The Techniques
Little Miss Understanding	Contours
Here I Go Again	Archie Bell and The Drells
Out On The Floor	Doby Gray
Real Humdinger	J J Barnes
Um, Um, Um, Um, Um	Major Lance
You Wan' It, You Got It	Detroit Emeralds
Wade In The Water	Ramsey Lewis
Zing Went The Strings Of My Heart	Trammps
Bernard, Pretty Purdy	Fickle Finger Of Fate
Cowboys To Girls	Sweet Blindness
Just A Rumour Baby	Isley Brothers
There's Gonna Be A Showdown	Archie Bell and The Drells
Step By Step	Joe Simon
Love On A Mountain Top	Robert Knight
Stop Her On Sight	Edwin Starr
Move On Up	Curtis Mayfield

Chapter 8

Queen's Hall Leeds

On the following Friday, after our weekend away in Manchester, the five of us Phil, Dave, TD, Yogi and I didn't have much to do so we all went to the Cali. It was as if the venue didn't want us to leave or we didn't want to leave the venue. It was such a brilliant place in its day, we would keep clocking in to see if the quality of the place was improving but it wasn't. In our eyes the Cali was going downhill rapidly. Quite a few of the regulars had stopped going and now the venue was too big for the amount of people that were attending. Instead of being the place that we would live and die for, it was a place we went to if we had nothing better to do.

Still at least we had lots of room to practice our new style dance steps when the DJ played the appropriate records. An upbeat Motown tune, Donnie Albert's 'Where Did Our Love Go', or 'Little Piece Of Leather' even 'Step By Step' by Joe Simon had the right type of beat to practice hovering in a three-foot circle.

We all thought, where the hell were we going to find a place as good as the Cali with the appropriate dance music? Also our little crew was drifting apart, Phil and Dave seemed to be more interested in the local pubs than searching for the real music we all loved. We all appeared to be at loose ends, plenty of energy and not enough places to go, until the day Yogi and I both saw an ad in *Black Music* magazine. It said the Leeds Soul Festival—possible live acts such as: Sam and Dave, Bob and Earl, Major Lance etc. at the Queen's Hall Leeds. Also it announced it was on all night and I mean *all* night—until the next morning.

I wasn't with Yogi when I found the ad. I was on a train coming back from shopping in Soho. On my way to London I picked up a soul mag called *Black Music*. It was as good as *Blues & Soul* and I thought to myself, "Not another standing order."

When I arrived at my favourite Soho record shop, an LP caught my eye. On the cover it had a massive black bloke with four lovely mini women standing in the palm of his hands. The LP was called *I've Got So Much To Give* by Barry White. I didn't normally buy records by the picture on the cover, but in this case I did, and I was not disappointed. The chap in the record shop sold me the LP for £1.25 as it was a year old. I thought to myself, 'Why didn't I know this artist?' On the train home I looked at the tracks on the LP and noticed 'Standing In The Shadows Of Love'. I wondered if it was the same as the Four Tops number and if it is, would it be as good? Then I browsed the *Black Music* mag again and thought if I take out another standing order, it is going to be another 25p a month. Oh, what the hell. I had to order it even though I struggled to read.

When I got home, the family was out so I ran a bath and placed *I've Got So Much To Give* on the record deck. I played the LP with more volume than I was normally allowed. While soaking in the bath and listening to my LP I thought this first track has got a long intro. It started with a plunking of the piano, violins then the haunting sound of the oboe, then different instruments started entering the equation—all the instruments seemed to increase pace. The women sang the words "*Standing in the Shadows of Love*" then there's a rough husky groan, the orchestra hit its full crescendo and Barry White starts to sing, "*I want to run but there's nowhere to go, heartaches will follow me I know,*" and so on...

I could not believe my ears! I dived out the bath with nothing on, skidded along the lino on the landing and placed the needle back to the start. Then I dived back in the bath to get warm again. What an LP it turned out to be. I put this one in the same category as *Three Hundred And Sixty Degrees* by Billy Paul, and *Understanding* by Bobby Womack. It was that good.

I thought, "What have I found?" When I played the flip side I was amazed. The track 'I've Got So Much To Give' kicked in, it just blew me away. I was so engrossed in my new LP by the time I thought about phoning Yogi about the ad, it was too late in the evening and had to wait till Sunday—anyway Liverpool were on *Match of the Day*.

The following day Yogi phoned me up quite early to say he'd found an advert in a new soul mag. called *Black Music*. Before he read out the details I said, "The Queen's Hall, Leeds." You might think this sounds a bit spooky but that kind of thing was happening all the time, especially when buying concert tickets or records. You see we were both looking out for the same thing. We even had the same taste in girlfriends—to the extreme that when Yogi married our Lorraine, she was the girl I adored when we were kids and will till the day I die! So it was not unusual to be thinking about the same things at the same time. Spooky eh?

We phoned the rest of the crew and all five of us were up for it. We had no idea what to expect. All we knew was that, in a venue over two hundred miles away the music we loved was being performed and played, so that was good enough for us.

Once Yogi had secured the tickets the excitement took over. Our conversations went like this:

"I wonder if the dance floor is as good as the Cali?"

"I bet it's held in a massive working men's club, they have those kind of places up North."

"I wonder if they sell mushy peas and meat pies. It's bound to have a Bistro bar."

"We might have to take a case or bag with some spare clothes if we're up all night."

Thank God we took sports-type holders—as it happens we would have looked right wallies with suitcases. We even spoke about what clothes to wear; our fashion at the Cali was a baggy high-waisted trouser and bowling shirts. Yogi and I had our own personalised bowling shirts—the colour was like a kingfisher blue with yellow vents. On the back of Yogi's was, of course, an embroidered Yogi Bear and on mine was the international soul logo, black fist with the words California Ballroom, two palm trees and underneath it said, 'Our kid Reg'.

After what seemed weeks and weeks of waiting, the soul festival finally arrived. We all loaded our bags into Yogi's van and off we went. We thought Caister was miles away from Hemel Hempstead, but Leeds was twice as far. It took ages to get there and we had at least four pee stops. We never used to worry how long it took to get to places and although there were five of us in a small van, we were comfortable.

TD, the small Fijian lad, worked at an upholsterer called Hukes in Hemel Hempstead. Forty years later and the shop is still there, in fact last year they renewed the seat on my Vespa. TD was an apprentice at Hukes and managed to get some foam rubber, which was roughly the size of the van floor. So you had a choice; sit in the front with Yogi or have a sleep in the back and that's how it was.

After hours of travelling, we finally arrived at the Queen's Hall Leeds. Nothing like we were expecting. Instead of a posh Northern nightclub, it was more like a massive aircraft hanger. We sat in the van for a few minutes, gobsmacked. We knew we were at the right place 'cos there were hundreds of Soulies queuing to get in. We were quite relieved by the sight. Most, if not all, of the men were wearing high waisted baggy trousers and some were wearing bowling shirts. To our amazement, they were taking their overnight bags into the venue, so we followed suit and fitted in perfectly.

Once inside, we were in bewilderment. The dance floor was solid concrete with large metal sheets. There were stalls selling sew-on patches, records or T-shirts and about four serving hatches. Two were drinks bars, one was selling cups of tea and coffee and one (as predicted) was selling meat pies with mushy peas—we did laugh.

There was a large stage with massive speakers on the sides, but what impressed me most, were the dancers. Some of them were dancing like the two Stoke lads that we had seen at the Top Rank in Watford, hovering in circles wearing one black glove and there were some dancers wearing black gloves on both hands. The gloves weren't just fashion accessories; they were for protection. These dancers weren't just hovering, they were gymnasts doing all kinds of tricks; back drops, front drops, handstands and a Cossack-type dance, where one leg was going round in a circle while balancing on alternate hands and when the leg came round the hands were switched. No wonder they wore gloves—they were hitting the concrete with such impact, without them their hands would have been smashed to bits. And this was not all. The dancers I liked watching were the ones that glided across the floor and then all of a sudden they were spinning like an ice skater—not just one or two spins, it was about six, and they rarely moved from the spot they started spinning on. Now and then, the dancers would put talcum powder on the floor. When I asked about the talc, a dancer said, "It's to stop the friction between the concrete floor and my leather-soled shoes."

When you watch one or two dancers it's good, but when you watched a couple of hundred, it was unbelievable—absolutely breathtaking. Also the sewn on patches weren't only on their clothes, they were all over their overnight bags and holdalls. It was a sort of symbol. Each patch represented the different soul clubs the soul dancer had visited. At the Leeds soul club, I bought three soul patches. One was JJ Barnes, one was Major Lance and the other was the same Torch patch that the two Stoke lads had worn on their shirts at Watford.

I also bought three records 'Manifesto' by James Lewis and The Case Of Time, 'Sking In The Snow' by Invitations, and the other was 'Don't Cry' By Melba Moore. These records were in the top five at the time with "Skiing in the Snow" being Number One. This was also the first time I had ever paid a pound for a seven-inch single. I had no idea that some of the records sold for an awful lot more money.

It was at this point I realised what Steve Schubert meant when I first ever went up the youth club.

He had told me, "If ever you collect records Reg, look after them. Especially if they are rare!"

RECORDS BOUGHT AROUND THIS TIME

I've Got Something Good	The Explosions
Satisfy Me Baby	The Sweets
That's The Way He Is	Ann Perry & M Davis
Ten Miles High	David and The Giants
Breakaway	The Steve Karmen Big Band
Help Me Find A Way	The Detroit Shakers
My Sugar Baby	Connie Clark Orchestra
Can't Help Loving That Man	Ila Van
Afternoon On The Rhino	Mike Post
Countdown Here I Come	The Tempos
Serenade	The Sounds Of Lane
Living In Love	Sheila Anthony
Bok To Bach	Fathers Angels
Super Love	David and The Giants
Strings A Go Go	Bobby Wilson
They're Talking About Me	Johnny Bragg
Sidra's Theme	Instrumental
I'll Always Need You	Dean Courtney
Cigarette Ashes	Jimmy Conwell
The Right Track	Billy Butler
Supertime	The Golden World Strings
Can't Help Loving You	Paul Anka
Manifesto	James Lewis Case Of Time
Don't Cry	Melba More
Try A Little Harder	The Fi-dels
Temptation Walk	Mirwood Strings
Thumb A Ride	Earl Wright

Chapter 9

Next Stop the Catacombs

After going to the Leeds Soul Festival, none of the local nightclubs could live up to our expectations. The music was like the stuff being played in the pop records chart and the dancers weren't a patch on those we had seen. We all felt a bit special really; it was as if we were called to this brilliant underground soul scene. I suppose if you search hard enough for something, one day you will eventually find it and that's what had happened.

Oh! How I thank God for stumbling across the *Blues & Soul* and the *Black Music* magazines. These magazines were the key to our new ventures. There were always a couple of ads for the Northern Soul scene. After reading some of the write-ups on the different clubs, we quite fancied visiting the Catacombs in Wolverhampton. From where we lived, Wolverhampton was just about two hours drive.

So we set off one Saturday afternoon. We were under no illusion as to what we might find—an old aircraft hanger, working mens' club or a dance hall. Who knew? Who cared? If the right music and the dancers were there, it could be held in an old workhouse for all we cared. Yeah! You've got it—that's what it looked like and it was brilliant!

The venue was in a road called Temple Street. An old brick building with arches above the windows, exactly like an old workhouse. Inside, "the Cats" appeared to be quite a cosy place with low ceilings and small alcoves with seating in them, but the best bit was the sound of the music. It seemed to travel hauntingly through all the nooks, crannies and archways. When you entered the Cats you could hear the music but you couldn't see where the sound was coming from until you walked to the far end of the building where there was a smallish dance floor. It wasn't until you stood on the dance floor that you could see the DJ, who was situated in another small alcove.

The Catacombs was one of the best places I had the privilege of going to, it was unique. With all these little cave-like alcoves, I have never seen anything like it and I doubt if I will ever again. The first time we went to the Cats, there were about forty people in the building. This was quite a good crowd as it was only a small place. There were three soul dancers that stood out above the rest. Their names were Squeak, Jethro and Sammy—Squeak and Jethro (the white guys) being the best spinners I have ever seen, and Sammy, a black chap who in my opinion was what a soul dancer was all about. He spun, glided and could do all the tricks; but in fairness, all three dancers were unbelievable. I just stood and tried to take in what I was seeing. How they moved, spun and dropped on the floor all in perfect time with the music. Just thinking about it still sends tingles down my arms and shivers down my spine. The place, the music and the dancers were that good.

We were all having a brilliant night until about ten thirty when 'All Of A Sudden, (Jeanette Williams) Sammy, Jethro and Squeak and about twenty others picked up their soul holdall bags and left the building.

"I wonder what's up," I said to Yogi.

"I don't know, I'll try and find out."

Yogi went to the DJ stand. Playing at the time was a DJ called Pep. Yogi was speaking with him for about half an hour. When he finally came back to where we were dancing, he had a massive smile on his face.

"Well," I said, "Where have they gone?"

"Not only have I found out where they've gone, I've ordered an EMI disc."

"What's an EMI disc?" I said.

"Well Reg," Yogi replied, "because the records are rare and so few and far between, the only way the likes of you and me can get the sounds, is on a taped cassette or on an EMI disc. I've ordered one of the instrumental of... wait for it... My Sugar Baby by The Connie Clark Orchestra."

"You're joking me, I love that sound," I said, "How much was that?"

"You don't wanna know Reg, a lot of money," Yogi said. "EMI discs are normally a fiver, but I'm having Pep's for three quid. Pep reckons the original is normally about fifteen."

"Really?" I said. "So how much is it going to take to get the others we want?"

"Well Reg, if you want the sound, 'You've Got To Pay The Price'" (Al Kent)

So engrossed in the education we were getting on records I almost forgot to ask Yogi about where the other dancers had gone.

"Oh, by the way," he said, "there's a new soul club opened called Wigan Casino and that's where all the dancers have gone."

"What you mean they've left a place as good as this to go there? I bet they all come back in half an hour."

"Oh no they won't, it's about another hundred miles away."

"It must be an all-night job then."

"You've got it Reg, the doors open at 2am and it must be good because when Pep has finished here he's going too."

"Here we go again," I thought. I sort of sensed where we were going next week by the excitement in Yogi's eyes.

On our way out, the organisers were selling soul patches that summed up the whole experience of the Catacombs. The patch was a man ship-wrecked on an island with a small boat, a cave and a little dog and cat. In a few weeks, we had bought records for over a pound each, had an EMI disc made, and put three soul club badges on our holdalls. Two of the clubs on the badges we had been to, and the other was the Golden Torch, which to this day we still regret not going to and always will. We've got the patches, the membership cards and the *Major Lance Live at the Torch* LP, but with great sadness we never walked through the doors of the building. Although we missed the Torch, we were so thankful we had found this underground soul scene and Yogi was determined we weren't going to miss many more clubs playing this music with our type of people, mostly hard working lads and lassies who live for the weekend soul clubs with a passion you would die for.

RECORDS BOUGHT AROUND THIS TIME

You Don't Love Me	Moses Smith
Nothing Can Compare To You	Velvet Satins
We Go Together	August & Deneen
If You Ever Walk Out Of My Life	Dena Barnes
My Sugar Baby	Connie Clark
At Last	Temprees
Out Of My Mind	Rain With Charity Brown
Tainted Love	Gloria Jones
Condition Red	Baltimore & Ohio Marching Band
The Night	Frankie Valli & The 4 Seasons
Girl Don't Make Me Wait	Bunny Sigler
Love Bandit	Kenya Collins
Night Owl	Bobby Paris
Breakaway Part Ii	Steve Karmen Band & Jimmy Radcliffe
Free For All	Phillip Mitchell
I Hear A Symphony	The Carmel Strings
Lord What's Happening To Your People?	Kenni Smith
I Don't Want To Discuss It	Little Richard
I Never Knew	Eddie Foster
That Beatin' Rhythm	Richard Temple
Come On Train	Don Thomas
It's Too Late	Bobby Goldsboro
What	Judy Street
Reaching For The Best	Exciters
Unsatisfied	Lou Johnson
The Snake	Al Wilson

Chapter 10

Wigan Casino, Blackpool Mecca and the Howard Mallet

The night the five of us (Yogi, Dave, Phil, TD and me) first went to Wigan Casino, we went via the Blackpool Mecca.

The weekend started on the Friday night with a trip to the Howard Mallet Soul Club in Cambridge. This was held at a youth club type place not dissimilar to the Square One Youth Club in Adeyfield, quite a modern place with a friendly atmosphere. The regulars were so enthusiastic to make you feel welcome and not intimidated.

We were greeted with questions like:

"Where are you from lads?"

"Do you collect sounds/records?"

"Have you been to many other soul clubs?"

"What do you think of ours?"

"Have you bought a patch yet? They are for sale by the door where you came in."

"What's your favourite record? Bet our DJ Tony Dellar has got it." and so it went on.

All five of us bought a patch for our soul bags and it was the biggest patch we ever purchased. There was what appeared to be two hammers crossed exactly like the West Ham football team's crest, and like many soul patches the Howard Mallet's was round. A black piece of felt approximately 5 inches in diameter, two crossed mallets in the centre and the words Howard Mallet Soul Club Cambridge around the outside. As the patch was so big, I decided to put mine on a tee shirt.

This soul club opened our eyes a bit. It was different to the other clubs we had been to recently. It was quite a nice place instead of being held in an old dilapidated building and was ideal for us. A place where you could start the weekend or somewhere we could take some of the people from where we lived, as a taster to this strange soul scene we had found. The music was top dollar and the sound system was crystal clear—so clear it helped us learn the words to our favourite records.

My top four 'choons' from the Mallet were: 'Panic' by Reperata and The Delrons; 'Too Late' by Bobby Goldsboro; 'They're Talking About Me' by Johnny Bragg and 'Living In Love' by Sheila Anthony.

Leaving the Mallet and bound for Blackpool, all five of us agreed we were going to be regulars at the Howard Mallet soul club. It was such a nice place, quite close (56 miles) to Hemel Hempstead compared to most of the other Northern Soul clubs. Travelling to the Mallet only took about an hour, easy to get to, great people and brilliant sounds!

During that Saturday in Blackpool we all took things really easy; chilling out at its best. Some slept in the van whilst others strolled around the town looking for record shops, or relaxing in a deckchair by the beach. We had to take it easy because Wigan Casino opened at two o'clock in the morning as it was an all-nighter, and the Mecca like a normal club—8 till late but not all night. So the plan was to go to the Mecca till midnight, then travel to Wigan.

We all met back at the van around 7pm and started to get ready. Yogi deliberately parked the van by the public toilets. Although there weren't many washbasins in there, it didn't take us long to wash and freshen up for the night ahead of us. Yogi suggested we wore smart strides and a collared shirt as he had an inkling that you might have to dress smarter to get in the Mecca. In my case I wore my baggy brown high waisters, an ice-blue Fred Perry and my dark blue Harrington jacket, (well I thought I looked good enough anyway).

When the five of us got to the Mecca and could see the people queuing to get in, we realised how smart you had to be. The Blackpool Mecca Soulies were really dressed well; they were as sharp as razors. Most of the lads wore tailor-made suits and the girls wore the most fashionable clothes I had ever seen. Leather coats and funky type skirts like those being worn in the London clubs that we had been to; they were one step ahead of the type of fashion that we had seen in the other Northern Soul clubs. They were obviously influenced not only by the skinheads' way of dressing but the way the Mods used to dress as well. They were really smart and as cool as cucumbers.

When we got to the entrance, the doorman said in a broad northern accent, "Hey, you can't come in like that lads, I don't mind the little lad wearing a windjammer but you must wear a shirt and tie to get in. What you do in that Highland Room is down to you but to get in, you must wear a tie."

"Do you sell ties," I said.

"No we don't," he laughed, "but worra good idea! I might just buy some for next week, but as for tonight, I'm sorry lads and I don't know where you're gonna get one either."

So that was it.

When we arrived back at the car, Dave, Phil and TD were sitting on a park bench thinking how we could kill time waiting for the Casino to open.

Yogi and I went for a piss. Spontaneously we both tore a length of toilet roll off, it was that cheap stuff that hurts your bum when you use it. You know the type. I think it has Izal in a green triangle in the corner of every sheet and it smelt like fucking pine trees. We both started to fold the paper along in long lengths. As I was wearing a Fred Perry, I tried to fold my paper in a half-inch strip then, carefully using a Royal Windsor knot, I made the dearest little mod tie you ever did see. As Yogi was wearing a proper shirt, he folded his paper in a two-inch strip before carefully putting his paper tie round his neck.

Standing on tiptoe looking in the mirror, which I could just about see I said, "What you reckon Yogi?"

"We look the bollocks, Son," Yogi replied,

We both strolled outside and shouted in our made up northern accents, "Ain't yer coming tut Mecca lads?" The other three took one look at us, then ran into the loo and proceeded to make their top of the range Blackpool Mecca ties.

This time, when we got to the door a different guy said, "Alright Lads, how many of you? Five? No problem, in you come boys," and as the Northerners say we were all "made up".

Inside the Mecca, if I can remember rightly, there was an escalator. Once at the top you strolled past the main ballroom to the Highland Room. Inside, it was done out in a Scottish theme with some tartan patterns on the walls and a really good dance floor. The bar was quite long and we got served with our drinks pretty quickly, then we noticed some of the lads had removed their ties, one had even removed his shirt as well! Most of the dancers were dressed really smart like they did in the London clubs down South. There were only a few in baggy trousers and bowling shirts. The Highland Room was more of a trend-setting place—it seemed a bit posh for a Northern Soul venue and I'm sorry to say I only went the once. I wasn't bowled over by the place like I had been by the Catacombs. This type of venue was similar to the ones we visited in our early soul days; it had nothing like the impact that I got from walking into the Cats. Also, I think everything was happening too fast for us. Within a few weeks, we had been to four different soul clubs, whereas in the past, once we had found a venue the five of us were happy with, we became regulars.

The Northern Soul scene was a lot different. The Soulies seemed to get a buzz from the number of different clubs they had been to and the amount of patches on their bags. The best bit of the Mecca was the music—the sounds were outstanding. There was the weirdest record I'd ever heard by the Commodores called "The Zoo", and the brilliant, brilliant sound of the Carstairs' "It Really Hurts Me Girl"—probably the best 'choon' ever, in my opinion.

Others that turned my head were "Contact" by The Three Degrees and a record called "Paris Blues" by Tony Middleton. As I only went to the Mecca for a few hours this is all I can say. The venue had songs to die for but a bit too posh for what we were looking for at the time.

As the night was coming to an end at the Mecca, the Soulies started changing from their posh suits to more casual looking clothing (maybe they had travelled a long distance and didn't want to crease their tailor-made clothes). Some of the lads were only changing their strides, replacing the parallel-style trouser with their baggy high-waisters and leaving their suit jackets on. By this time there weren't many ties being worn at all.

The five of us got back to the van ready for our trip to 'The Casino'. The whole affair still seemed strange to us, leaving a venue after midnight and instead of going home to bed we were on our way to the next do. Weird!

Just as we were leaving Blackpool we noticed a chap thumbing a lift. He was wearing a bottle green suit jacket with baggy corduroy trousers and carrying a holdall covered with soul patches. Yogi pulled over and asked the chap where he was going.

"I'm on my way to Wigan Casino."

"So are we," Yogi said. "Jump in and you can tell us how to get there as we've never been before. What's your name?"

"Steve; I'm from Preston."

After speaking with Steve for about five minutes, I realised we were going somewhere really special. I told Steve this was only our second all-nighter, the other being the Leeds Soul Festival and he said, "You're gonna love it at Wigan."

"What's your favourite record Steve," I said.

"'Manifesto'." he said.

"What's the best dance floor you have ever danced on?"

Without any hesitation he replied, "Wigan Casino."

I enquired which club had the best atmosphere—once again his answer was "Wigan Casino." I thought to myself, wow, we're going to be there in a couple of hours.

"What about the sounds? Where's the best sounds being played at the moment?"

Steve looked at me and said, "Fockin' Wigan Casino, the best dance floor, best atmosphere and best sounds." (In Steve's opinion—could heaven ever be like this?) "Have you got membership cards, lads?"

"Yes," Yogi said, "Reg and I sent off about three weeks ago."

"Only if you haven't, I do know the manager," Steve replied, "but it's good you've already got them. When we get to the Casino, I'll disappear and meet you inside, as I have some business to deal with, if you know what I mean…"

When Steve had gone I said to the lads, "That's strange. What a nice bloke to be having some business to deal with." (In London that's fighting talk—when someone's upset you, you're going to deal with it). It wasn't until about a month later I found out what he meant, and what he meant was 'I've got to get some 'Jack & Jill's' to help me stay awake all night!' A lot of the sayings meant different things. You see we were Londoners in the week and Northerners at weekends so it took a while to get our heads around it all. On numerous occasions Yogi, being a Mancunian, had to explain what our Northern friends meant.

When we arrived in the car park, there were already two coaches parked up. You could see Wigan Casino from the car and what a sight it was, too. It was one o'clock in the morning and the Soulies were as fresh as daisies. Everyone had an element of excitement about them, standing in small groups chattering away like magpies.

It took no time at all, for the lads and me to get ready. Yogi handed out the membership cards in case we got split up and off we went. It was brilliant just standing outside. Everyone was friendly and happy, the tingles had already started in my arms and you got an instant buzz just walking past the main door. We walked through a door, which was the entrance to a café-type place. Two lads were playing some sounds and about half a dozen Soulies were dancing. I've read books recently calling this café 'Jokers' but we knew it as the 'Beachcomber'. I really loved it in the Beachcomber especially if there were a couple of lads DJ-ing before or after the all-nighter.

After a quick cup of tea, we started queuing to get in the main building. In the very early days of Wigan Casino the queue was not very big, but it only took a couple of months and then it was like going to a local derby football match—the queue was massive. I can still hear the late Mike Walker insisting that we would all get in, if we "STOPPED PUSHING!" Once through the door, you went up some stairs and paid a very nice old lady one-pound entrance fee, then you went up some more stairs and through a door to the main room. The thing I remember most was a stale smell of Brut aftershave, the heat and the pounding dance floor. As you walked across it, it seemed to bounce as if it was spring loaded—and yes it was!

Looking up from the dance floor, the balcony was shaped like a giant horseshoe, with the open end being where the stage was. Large wooden columns held up the balcony and there were the most amazing Victorian patterns in plaster. The whole experience of the place was overwhelming.

The five of us went upstairs to the balcony and peered over, looking down on the dancers. It was like a sea of people all dancing in time to the beat of the record then all of a sudden a dancer would wind up ready for a spin. An opening would appear in the sea of people while the dancer performed the ice skating spin. When a dancer finished spinning, the gap would close up. Gaps would also appear when the dancers performed their tricks; backdrops, jumps, splits etc. With so many dancers moving at the same time, it was inevitable they would bump into each other now and then. When this happened there was no malice; it would be a quick touch of the hand in acknowledgement and everyone just carried on dancing.

Looking around on the balcony, groups of Soulies would be gathering around small tables. Sitting at the tables would be other Soulies selling or swapping records. Wads of money were changing hands right left and centre. Then we noticed some soul fans had battery cassette recorders, taping sounds with their microphones dangling over the edge of the balcony. Before we went to Wigan we were told about people recording the records they couldn't afford, so I had taken my own cassette recorder with a built-in mike. Once we had found a spare table as a space where we could leave our holdalls, I just left my own cassette recorder running until the tape was finished.

As I'm writing this page, it is thirty-three years later and somewhere in my little cottage I still have that tape cassette. When we were recording, a brilliant song came on called 'You Made Me This Way' by Ila Vann. In the middle of the record, there is an instrumental interlude and in a 'London-Northern' accent you hear Dave ask TD for the time and TD saying, "The time is half past two-ooo."

So all these years later, we can still re-live those treasured memories. We were all having such a brilliant time, the next thing we knew it was the morning.

They played the famous last two—'Time Will Pass You By' by Tobi Legend; and 'I'm On My Way' by Dean Parish. I might be wrong but I believe 'Long After Tonight' by Jimmy Radcliffe was added a few months later, making the world-renowned, famous last three.

Everyone started clapping, the night was over—and what a night it was...

Walking back to the van, we noticed some of the soul fans were heading for the local swimming pool for a swim or a shower and others to the corner shop for a pint of milk. On the drive back there was plenty spoke about the whole weekend, and all five of us decided that Wigan Casino was going to replace our beloved Cali, even though we had to travel 400 miles to get there and back. When we were discussing the music we found quite a lot of the sounds we liked were instrumentals, brilliant up-tempo sounds. We had no idea that within the next few months the most dynamic lyrics would be added. Also you will notice that some of the song titles which accompany this chapter, are 'cover up' names, where they disguised the real name of the tune. This kept them top sounds for a lot longer.

RECORDS BOUGHT AT THIS TIME

Better Use Your Head	Little Anthony & The Imperials
Crazy Baby	The Coasters
You Don't Say A Word	Yvonne Baker
Let Her Go	Otis Smith
Cool Off	Detroit Executives
Please Stay	The Ivories
What Shall I Do	Frankie and The Classicals
Daylight Saving Time	Keith
If You Ask Me	Jerry Williams
Cashing In	The Voices Of East Harlem
I'm Gonna Change	The Velours
Blowing My Mind To Pieces	Bob Relf
Let Our Love Grow Higher	Eula Cooper
Please Operator	Tony & Tyrone
Breakout	Mitch Ryder & The Detroit Wheels
I Really Love You	The Tomangoes
I'm Com'un Home In The Morn'un	Lou Pride
You've Been Away	Rubin
Where Is The Love?	Betty Wright
Send Him Back	Pointer Sisters
Panic	Reparata and The Delrons
You Gotta Pay Your Dues	The Drifters
You Don't Know Where Your Interest Lies	Dana Valery
Too Late	Larry Williams/ Johnny Watson
Love You Baby	Eddie Parker
Help Yourself	Jimmy James & The Vagabonds

Chapter 11

Wigan Casino, Benbo's and the Heavy Steam Machine

The next time Yogi and I went to Wigan Casino, it was just the two of us, as Phil, Dave and TD were doing something different on this particular weekend. We arrived at the Casino around about midnight so we had plenty of time to chill out. We met a really nice couple called Steve and Margaret from Bradford and as usual we got talking about the sounds. I asked Margaret what was her favourite sound at the moment.

"'Surrounded By A Ray Of Sunshine' by Samantha Jones," she replied, "What's yours Reg?"

I said, "There's so many, but there is one I quite like it's by Bobby Goldsboro. I believe it's called 'Too Late'. I heard it first at the Howard Mallet."

"Oh that's a great song Reggie, I love it too."

It was so strange Yogi and I had met this couple that we had never seen before and in about twenty minutes we felt that we had known them all our lives. Steve had a cassette tape he wanted to play to Yogi, so we went and sat in Steve's car. Steve and Yogi were in the front and Maggie and I were in the back. Steve had some magnificent sounds on his tape cassette—'choon' after 'choon', the sounds were dancing around Steve's small car but it wasn't just an education in the music that I was going to get on this particular occasion!

Maggie tapped Steve on the shoulder and in said, "Do you want owt tonight?"

Steve replied, "No, not really, I'm going to be talking about the sounds with Yogi. You and Reg just look after yourselves." Maggie opened a tin of Coca Cola. In a polythene bag there were small wraps of tissue paper just like the blue salt wraps you got in the Smith's 'Salt Your Own' crisps.

Maggie said, "Swallow this Reg, and quickly have a drink of coke." so I did about five times, it tasted bloody awful then this vile taste kept repeating. After about five or ten minutes, Maggie gave me a stick of chewing gum then straight away she said, "You better have another; you're gonna need it."

So I'm sitting in the back of the car with a mouth full of chewing gum. "Is this to hide the vile taste?" I said.

"No," Maggie laughed. "It's to stop you biting your bloody tongue off!"

The pair of us couldn't stop laughing—then it happened. The music got clearer and clearer and tingles started going up and down my arms; my tiredness of travelling so far just drifted away. Maggie tapped Steve on the shoulder again and said, "Reg and me are ready to go in now. Can we go?"

"Alright," said Steve, "but there are still some sounds I want Yogi to hear, so if we pop out during the night you'll know where we are."

"Okay," said Maggie, "I doubt if I'll know you're gone, I'll be too busy dancing with Reg."

I quickly informed Maggie that I wasn't that good, I'm just learning, I do more watching than dancing.

"Not tonight Reg," said Maggie. "We'll dance to every record played."

"STOP PUSHING AT THE BACK."

On the dance floor, it seemed even more amazing than it did a couple of weeks before. Maggie quickly found a table and we all put our soul bags down to mark our spot.

"No watching tonight Reg, we'll dance over there."

I turned round to tell Yogi that Maggie and I were going to dance,

Yogi's reply was, "Really, what straight away? You mind how you go. Steve and I will have a good laugh watching! If I'm not here when you come off the floor, I'll be on the balcony looking for sounds with Steve."

Maggie and I probably started dancing about quarter to three and we only left the floor for a pee or to catch our breath. Now and then, Yogi and Steve would pass us a Coke, or a glass of water, but that's all we would stop dancing for. Apart from just 'hovering in three-foot circles' I tried everything—spins, backdrops, splits etc. I wasn't very good at the acrobatic-type dancing but I did like the spinning. Our clothes were wringing with sweat and we changed our tops on at least three occasions. I had never danced so much in all my life. I was even getting the odd nod from the likes of Sammy and Jethro, (Soulies who I idolised, especially when they were dancing). I didn't know if the nods were "what the hell is that fool doing over there" or "he's doing alright for a beginner." All I knew was I had a lot more confidence and I had a feeling of acceptance from the floor so that was good enough for me.

When the night was over we did the normal; swim, shower, down the pool, pint of milk from the corner shop and a cup of tea. In my case, bottles of Lucozade—as you do! But instead of going straight home from the Casino we made a small detour to Bradford where Steve and Maggie lived because, you've guessed it, Steve wanted to show us his records. We only stayed for about half an hour, but in that short space of time we heard some of the best sounds around and we had truly met two really nice friends.

On the way home, the downside of the experience started to kick in; I was absolutely shattered and every now and then I got the most horrendous cramp in my legs. Also I had a splitting headache. The body had been overworked; all the muscles were aching so lord knows what damage the heart had been receiving!! I put it all down to experience (learning curves of life). I believe you have to try these things so you can advise your own offspring when they themselves are at the adventurous stages of their lives. Also as a parent you need to know the tale-tell signs; mood swings, dilated eyeballs, licking of the lips etc. I had to mention the downside in my story 'cos if I didn't I would be lying and that's it.

From the sounds I had heard the previous night in Wigan Casino, I had a new favourite. It's the sound of 'If You Ever Walk Out Of My Life' by Dena Barnes. The tune has a gentle northern type beat with a Minnie Ripperton-type voice over the top (brilliant 'choon'). Definitely on the wants list! As any Northern Soul fan will tell you, you could have half a dozen favourites but there is always one that sticks out from the rest, even if it is only your favourite for a short space of time.

The next couple of times we went to the Casino all five of us went, including one of my sister Jackie's best mates, Lorraine Hutt. So in Yogi's small van was Yogi, me, TD, Dave, Phil and Lorraine. Lorraine became a sort of motherly figure towards the lads and we all loved her. She sort of kept us in check and if one of us got a girlfriend she would give us about twenty reasons why we should not go out with this girl.

On one occasion when I got a girlfriend (I won't mention her name!) Lorraine said, "Well, I don't like her!"

I said, "What's the reason this time?"

Lorraine's reply was: "She looks a bit easy, can't comb her hair properly and she's got dirty ankles."

So you can see what the lads were up against. In truth I think we were Lorraine's lads and she didn't like other girls meddling on her patch.

After going to Wigan, the Cats and the Howard Mallet for a few months, we got to know quite a few Soulies who had the same opinion we did. Wigan was our favourite but there were a lot of other venues not to be ignored. Along with the Catacombs and Mallet, we started to visit the Heavy Steam Machine in Stoke on Trent. This club was held on a Sunday night so a full weekend was taken up. The only problem was what did we do whilst waiting for the weekend to come around to save suffering from withdrawal symptoms?

At the age nineteen or twenty, we went back to our local youth club and started to play this new music. After showing some of the younger members the dance moves, Bennetts End Soul Club (Benbos) was formed.

The first night the lads and I went back to Bennetts End Youth Club, I bet the members thought, 'What are these old geezers doing in our youth club?' We had about six precious record pressings with us along with Yogi's EMI disc of 'My Sugar Baby' (instrumental).

We gave the DJ the records and said, "Alright, mate. Play these in between some old Motown dance classics and we'll fill the dance floor for you."

So that's what Dave the DJ did. After about three or four records, the hardest of the club members, a lad called Chris Grace, walked onto the dance floor and started to dance; then some of the others followed suit. Yogi said to Chris, "You see it's not such a sissy thing for men to dance on their own is it?"

Now we had established ourselves back in the youth club, we desperately needed some more sounds and we needed them pretty quick. So to save more money we stopped travelling in Yogi's van to the casino and hitched a lift instead. Dave and Phil weren't 'souling' as much as Yogi, TD, Lorraine and me, so when the four of us were hitching to Wigan we split up in pairs. One pair was Yogi and TD, the other was Lorraine and me. It was a brilliant move on my part, as Lorraine was so good looking and we always got the first car to stop. At the entrance to the M1 in Hemel were some bushes where I would stand then I would tell Lorraine to hitch her frock up a bit and stick her thumb out, then in no time at all a car would stop to pick us up. If we left Hemel at Saturday lunchtime, we could nearly always guarantee we would be at Knutsford service station on the M6 between six to seven o'clock, where Yogi and T always took a little longer. Once you reached Knutsford it was no problem to get to 'The Casino' as all the Soulies that hired coaches would stop there for something to eat and give anyone travelling in the same direction a lift.

After a few weeks, some of the older youth club members asked us if we would take them to a real soul club. That's not saying our soul club was not real, as it was a great little soul club, they just wanted to see what was out there. So on Fridays we started taking some of the best dancers with us to the Howard Mallet. At first we took Chris Grace, Kev Keady, Lorraine Holland and Susan Hussey. As time went on we took different youth club members so they all got a turn. If I can remember rightly on one occasion, Yogi borrowed a mini bus from somewhere, (most probably the football team he was playing for) and we could take about a dozen with us. The Howard Mallet club was ideal to introduce young members to the Northern Soul scene, just as long as their mums and dads knew where they were going, and that we wouldn't be home until about one in the morning.

In the July of 1974, I believe it was Saturday the 13th, there was going to be the last all-nighter at the Catacombs. When we read the advert in *Blues & Soul*, Yogi and I were absolutely gutted, as the Catacombs soul club was so precious to us.

All I kept saying to Yogi was, "How can they shut the Cats? What on earth could be the reason to close such a brilliant club?"

"They're shutting it for redevelopment," Yogi replied. Then he said, "Reg, instead of being so upset, why don't we make the last night at the Cats be so brilliant."

"How are we going to do that?" I said.

"I'll try and borrow the mini bus again and we'll take some more people with us, it will be great. See who's interested and I'll sort out the transport and the tickets."

So that's what I did. The five lads and Lorraine were definitely up for it, then I asked Lorraine Holland and Sue Hussey. The day I spoke to them they had just received their new bowling shirts through the post. Sue and Lorraine asked if they could borrow my Catacombs soul patch because they wanted to embroider the logo on the back of their new bowling shirts—and I must say it looked brilliant when they had finished. It looked as if they had got hold of two giant Catacombs patches and sewn them on but I knew different—no such patches existed and they had created these works of art all by themselves. I also asked my sister Jackie if she wanted to go. In the end there were about ten of us altogether and off we went. When we arrived at the Cats, the queue to get in went right down the steps and along the pavement. Once we finally entered the venue, it was absolutely packed. You couldn't show the newcomers, such as my sister, the brilliance of the place as there were so many people and as for dancing, it was pretty limited. I quickly decided to myself it was going to be a listening night and I wasn't disappointed. The sounds were fabulous, 'choon' after 'choon', every one a gem.

The walls of the place were wringing wet, and this in turn made the floors wet; not too good for dancing, but the atmosphere was the best ever. As I knew this was going to be the last night of 'the Cats' I wanted to savour every minute of it and that is what I did right to the end.

I believe the DJ line up was:

Blue Max, Pep, Soul Sam, Keith Minshull, Russ Winstanley, Mick Fellow, and Bazel.

At the time Pep was my favourite but nowadays I lean towards Soul Sam as I like most of his modern sets. Before I knew it, this fabulous night was over and the last record I heard played in the Catacombs was 'Where Have All The Flowers Gone?' by Walter Jackson.

Then I bumped into Yogi who said, "Come with me, some people are getting souvenirs!"

Now I know it was only the gent's toilet door and only a cheap hardboard flush door (being a carpenter I'd know!) but it wasn't any old toilet door—it was the Catacombs door and that's what we got—two pieces of the gent's toilet door.

When we got home, Yogi gave me his piece of door and I carefully painted the Catacombs logo on them. Yeah you've guessed it, we both still own them to this day even when we've moved houses these two bits of hardboard have stayed with us, and they always will.

RECORDS BOUGHT AROUND THIS TIME

Happy	William Bell
I'm Getting On Life	Wombat
Picture Me Gone	Madeline Bell
The Love We Knew	Poppies
All Of A Sudden	Jeanette Williams
Papa Ooh Mow Mow	The Sharonettes
Put Me In Your Pocket	Jeanette Harper
Love Felling	Val Mckenna
My Hearts Symphony	Gary Lewis & The Playboys
Suspicion	Prophets
Exodus	Biddu
What A Difference A Day Makes	Esther Phillips
Love Don't You Go Through No Changes	Sister Sledge
Kiss Me Know	Florence Devore
Just Walk In My Shoes	Gladys Knight and The Pips
I'm Gonna Pick Up My Toys	Devonnes
I've Got Something Good	Sam And Kitty
I've Got The Need	The Moments
If I Had My Way	Troy Keyes
Ain't No Soul In These Old Shoes	Ronnie Milsap
You Touched Me	Judy Harris
Cochise	Paul Humphrey
Take A Letter Maria	Boots Randolph
Long After Tonight Is All Over	Jimmy Radcliffe
Time Will Pass You By	Tobi Legend
I'm On My Way	Dean Parrish

Chapter 12

Wigan Casino, Samantha's, Cleethorpes Pier

Just before the first anniversary at Wigan Casino, one of our local friends asked if he could come along with us. His name was Jon Buck.

I said to Jon, "You're having a laugh! How can we take you up north souling? Someone might recognise you! Every other Saturday, you get into trouble at football matches. What happens if we introduce you to someone that you were rucking with at Euston Station? In the Northern soul clubs we all get on with each other, whichever part of the country you come from. I really don't know Jon, I'll have to ask Yogi. I'll let you know if we are going Saturday."

Later that evening I met up with Yogi and said, "What do you reckon Yogi? Bucky wants to come to Wigan with us."

Yogi replied, "It'll be alright as long as he doesn't upset anyone. Tell him to be ready about 8'oclock. We'll go in the van and that will give him time to get home from watching the Arsenal. They're playing at Highbury, one of those closed season friendlies. I bet he's going, he doesn't miss many."

Yogi picked me up at 7.30pm, then we went round for Jon and as usual, although Jon was a bit of a tearaway, he looked dead smart. You know the type, one of those blokes that look good whatever they're wearing. On this occasion, Jon wore some baggy cords, a collared shirt and a Wrangler denim jacket. So he certainly dressed for the occasion and didn't look out of place.

Jon must have been planning to come to Wigan Casino with us for quite some time, because as soon as he got in the van he produced his brand new Casino membership card. He even had the white 'Keep the Faith' Wigan patch sewn on the pocket of his wrangler jacket!

All the time we were travelling, Jon was talking. The whole five hours he was asking, "What's it like, will they play 'Skiing In The Snow' or 'Out On The Floor'? I won't let you down. I'll behave myself. Are we nearly there yet?" and so on.

It wasn't until we pulled in to Knutsford Services that Jon stopped asking questions, he just looked in bewilderment and said, "Coaches? They come in coaches?"

"Yes Jon, they come in coaches. Loads of Soulies come to the Casino in coaches. We'll stop here for about half an hour Jon, have something to eat and see if some of our mates pull in."

"You've got mates this far away from Hemel."

"Yes Jon. Soulies are very friendly people, and in no time at all they will be your mates as well."

As we walked into the restaurant part of the service station Yogi said to Jon, "The coaches you saw in the car park are the ones from Bedford and Wolverhampton."

"How do you know that?"

"Well," said Yogi, "you've got Jethro, Sammy and the Wolverhampton lot sitting over there and Steve, Angie and Liz from Cannock with the Bedford crew a few tables down."

Steve from Bedford walked over and asked if we could get him a cup of tea, then said, "Do you want a lift in lads?"

"No thanks mate, we are in a car this week, but thanks anyway."

We introduced Jon to all the Soulies we knew, and after a little break we left for the last part of the journey. When we got back to the van all Jon could talk about was the Soulies he had just met. It was great watching someone getting the same buzz that Yogi and I got every time we went. He loved everything about the scene so much that within a few months he was running his own fifty-two seater coach to the Casino and this changed our means of transport once again. No more thumbing or hitching a lift for us. It was all aboard Buckie's coach from

Bennetts End to the Casino. Also, this meant you could get your head down on the way home for a couple of hours' sleep.

This in turn helped Yogi, as he was a brilliant footballer and if we got home in time he would go and play for his team, even after an all-nighter. When his team was playing on a Sunday morning, Yogi was torn between playing football and dancing. On the weekends when he played football and couldn't go to Wigan, I would go souling with Buckie. On one occasion at the Casino, Jon met a girl called Cheryl from Huddersfield and I was quite keen on her mate Debbie; their other friend was called Liz. They told us one of their favourite venues was Samantha's in Sheffield. Jon and I went a couple of times, it was quite posh, in other words it wasn't an old building, it was quite new and situated above the Silver Blades ice rink—well worth a visit but nothing like the Casino, which was, in my opinion, the heart of the scene with all the other clubs surrounding it.

The other Northern Soul club we were visiting around this time was at Cleethorpes. It was like being on your holidays, because the club was situated on the end of Cleethorpes Pier. I loved souling at this venue as it was so different. You queued on the pier with the old sea crashing against the pillars below you, your soul holdall in one hand and your plate of cockles in the other. For us townies, it was a day out at the seaside and it made a lovely change.

The first time I went to Cleethorpes wasn't so lovely though; it was another learning curve—never thumb a lift on your own! It all started when Jon said that he wanted to take Ann with us this time. (Ann was Jon's girlfriend in Hemel Hempstead, if you know what I mean.) So not wishing to hitch a lift on my own, I phoned Mandy who lived in Watford and she agreed to come with me; but when I got to her house she had another girl with her. We tried to thumb it with the three of us, but it wasn't gonna happen so we had to split up—it was the two girls together and me on my own.

To my amazement, the first car stopped for me, the driver asked where I was going. I said, "I'm going to Cleethorpes, if you could get me to Leicester it would help." As we were going up the M1 we got talking and the driver asked why I had so many badges on my bag. I told him I was in the Northern soul scene but unless you go and see for yourself you won't have a bloody clue. Then he told me he was in a type of scene.

"What's that then," I asked.

"I'm in the gay scene," he replied.

I was gob-smacked. I froze on the spot, but although I felt terribly uncomfortable, I quickly said, "Oh well; everyone to their own." It was awful after that, it went from two guys talking happily to a deadly silence and all I kept doing was looking at the road signs. I think the driver could sense how uncomfortable I was and at the next turn off he stopped. Although we were in the middle of nowhere and about ten miles from Leicester, I quickly got out the car and started running down this quiet country lane. I looked behind me, then the driver turned off and to my relief went down the motorway from where we had just come.

"What am I going to do now," I thought, "is searching for soul worth all this?"

I walked down the lane for about twenty minutes then hesitantly stuck my thumb out again. The only thing that came past me was an old tractor towing a hay cart. I thought 'just my luck', and then about fifty yards in front of me the bloody thing stopped.

When I walked along side the tractor the farmer said, "Where you going son?"

I couldn't believe it. I said, "I'm looking for a busier road as I'm hoping to get to Cleethorpes by midnight."

"Hop on the hay cart and I'll take you to the main road to Leicester," said the farmer. So there I was lying in the back of a hay cart with my Wigan bag beside me thinking to myself 'no ones gonna believe this!' I did finally reach Cleethorpes pier at about one thirty and after all that had happened that day I didn't do too badly.

I quickly found Jon, Ann and Mandy (Mandy's friend had only travelled with Mandy to visit her mother up north somewhere...)

"What took you so long?" Jon asked.

All I said was, "You don't want to know mate!"

Still, the night was brilliant and the floor was pounding most of the time. There was a sad moment in the evening when a Soulie asked the DJ to play 'Time Will Pass You By' by Tobi Legend for one of their friends who had died a couple of weeks prior to the event.

About six o'clock in the morning, Jon had bought a picture-sleeve copy of 'I Hear A Symphony' by The Carmel Strings, and I managed to get a copy of 'All Of A Sudden' by Jeanette Williams on a black Beat label—another tune crossed off my wants list. Then Mandy came up trumps, there was a lad there she knew from Watford who was willing to give us all a lift back home. So all in all it turned out to be a great night rounded off by the sound I purchased for £2.50.

When I look back on those good old days, although I went souling mostly with Yogi and Lorraine, I had some brilliant nights with Jon Buck. One of the best nights I had with Buckie was seeing Betty Wright live at Wigan Casino. Betty was a very powerful singer and really got the crowd going. Everyone was clapping to her songs and when she sang her Wigan favourite 'Where Is The Love?' the place went wild. Apart from Jackie Wilson, this was the best night at 'The Casino'.

Back home we found out lots of our friends from our skinhead days in the Hemel area were getting involved with the music. We were amazed when we found out kids as young as eleven were deep into this new soul music and loving every minute of it.

FAVOURITE RECORDS AT THIS TIME

Hit & Run	Rose Batiste
I'll Do Anything	Doris Troy
Hipit	Hosanna
Mighty Lover	The Mighty Lovers
Gonna Be A Big Thing	Yum Yums
Washed Ashore	Platters
Time's A Wasting	The Fuller Brothers
Love, Love, Love	Bobby Hebb
Try A Little Harder	The Fidels
Don't You Care Anymore	Jodi Mathis
She'll Come Running Back	Mel Britt
Surrounded By A Ray Of Sunshine	Samantha Jones
Oh My Darlin	Jackie Lee
One Wonderful Moment	The Shakers
Suspicion	Originals
If It's All The Same To You	Luther Ingram
Long Gone	Debbie Fleming
You Made Me This Way	Ila Vann
Love Trap	T D Valentine
Angel Baby	George Carrow
I Got The Fever	Creation
Are You Ready For This?	The Brothers
I Can't Do It	Eddie & Ernie
This Old Heart Of Mine	Tammi Terrell
You Don't Want Me No More	Major Lance
Do I Love You?	Frank Wilson

Chapter 13

Wigan Casino, Pioneer, St Ives

By Christmas of 1974, Bennetts End Soul Club was getting busier and busier and one Friday night Yogi really pushed the boat out by fetching the top disc jockey to our youth club. His name was Brian Rae. I don't know if Yogi had to pay him to come down to our club, but if he did, it would have been out of his own pocket and as far as I know he didn't. What I do know is Brian was very interested in Yogi's records by this time. Yogi and I had quite a few sounds, enough to run a small soul club in Bennetts End, or help out at the Pioneer in St. Albans, but that was it. So when Yogi brought Brian Rae into the equation with his records, this was the icing on the cake. More and more club members were approaching Jon Buck for tickets for his coach to Wigan Casino especially after listening to Brian's set.

When the night was over, Brian stayed at Yogi's house and the next day when Brian was leaving his last words to Yogi were, "Are you sure you don't want to sell that record Yogi?"

"Yes, I'm quite sure Brian."

After Brian had left I quickly asked Yogi, "What record was that then?"

"'Panic' by Reparta and The Delrons on a yellow Mala label." We were both delighted that one of us had a sound that a DJ of Brian's quality wanted.

My reply to Yogi was, "Whatever you do, don't sell it mate." I'm pleased to say Yogi still has the record to this day.

On the Saturday, Jon's coach was practically full and as time was getting on I asked Jon if there was a problem.

"Not really, I'll give it another five minutes. I'm waiting for another six lads from St. Albans; Barry McHugh, Trevor Jackson and some others."

As we were talking they arrived. Whilst we were travelling, the St. Albans lads were asking Yogi and I about our soul club, as they also had one of their own. It was in St. Albans, held at their youth club called the Pioneer, which was situated next to the fire station on the outskirts of the city. Their youth club was a lot bigger than ours and as it was out of the way from any houses it had great potential for an all-nighter, which was a massive plus for them. There was no way we could have an all-nighter at our youth club, but I do believe we had the better sounds.

As time went on and the St. Albans crew were using Buckie's coaches more often, we all became good friends. Then one day, Barry asked Yogi and me if we would like to play some of our 'choons' at the Pioneer club. We both felt quite honoured by this; we definitely had the right sounds all we had to do was learn how to use the equipment, which I found was not so easy. To this day I still find it quite difficult, but I do have some nice records.

On the night I was attempting to be a DJ, I did impress the floor with a couple of 'choons' I had; 'Better Use Your Head' by Marion Ryan, on a blue Phillips label, 'I Got The Vibes' by Joshie Jo Armstead on a green Gospel Truth and 'Mighty Lover' by cover name Mighty Lovers on a yellow Boogaloo. So all in all, I was happy with my efforts and the floor did clap between some of my records. After seeing what had happened between Hemel and St. Albans, I wondered if this was happening all over the country, where lads who were nearly twenty years of age were going back to their old youth clubs during the week, just to play their records and have a dance, whilst waiting for the weekend to come round. Even the Howard Mallet club in Cambridge reminded me of a youth club type place, which we were still visiting on a regular basis with the new recruits from our own soul club.

We also went to St. Ives near Cambridge. This soul club seemed to be the bigger venue for the Howard Mallet Soulies to go to when they weren't going to Wigan, Blackpool or places you had to travel miles to get to. Although we had loads of clubs we could visit, I still felt I was missing out on something, if I wasn't at 'The Casino' as it was still my favourite venue. To me it was a very special place and I still feel privileged to have been a part of it all.

In late June 1974, I strolled around to the youth club. I was earlier than usual and as I approached the club, someone was playing our records. As I walked in, to my amazement I discovered what you might call "the Carlsberg kids" (probably the best dancers in the world). The Townsend brothers, Peter, David and Simon, a young John Frazer and a skinny Peter Wickham were the 'under thirteen' youth club members.

Peter, the eldest of the Townsend brothers said, "Hey Reg, are we good enough for Wigan?"

"Of course you are," I said, "but you'll never get in, you're too young."

About two weeks later, Jon Buck ran another coach to the Casino. As we were approaching Northampton just past the Pete Wickham house (if you were going to Wigan at that time you will know exactly where I mean) three little heads popped up from under the seats! We had stowaways on board!

Little Pete said, "Don't take us back, please let us go, we'll sit outside all night with a cassette player if we have to. We just want to see the place."

Once again it was a brilliant night in 'The Casino'. First I went on the balcony and bought some records, then got on the floor early and tried to stop worrying about the boys outside.

I suppose you're wondering did the boys get in?

You bet your life! Dancing like they did, no one was going to throw them out, and from that day on they were probably the youngest Wigan members.

FAVOURITE RECORDS AT THIS TIME

There Was A Time	Gene Chandler
Tears Nothing But Tears	Lee Roye
The Zoo	The Commodores
He's So Irreplaceable	Doris Jones
Wanting You	April Stevens
Stay Close To Me	Five Stairsteps & Cubie
Girl You Better Wake Up	Liberty
I Love Music	O'Jays
I Don't Know What Foot To Dance On	Kim Tolliver
Hung Up On Your Love	Montclairs
Find My Way	Cameo
I Got The Vibes	Joshie Jo Armstead
I Can't Help Myself	Johnny Ross
Don't It Make You Feel Funky	Joe Hicks
Man Without A Woman	Michael & Raymond
You Hit Me Right Where It Hurts	Alice Clark
You Don't Mean It	Towanda Barnes
It Really Hurts Me Girl	The Carstairs
I Wanna Give You Tomorrow	Benny Troy
Lady, Lady, Lady	The Boogie Man Orchestra
Name It You Got It	Mickey Moonshine
Keep On Running Away	Bits'n'Pieces
Heaven In The Afternoon	Lew Kirton
Contact	The Three Degrees
Overture	The Miracles
It'll Never Be Over For Me	Timi Yuro

Chapter 14

No Chance

Yogi and I were going to Wigan as much as we possibly could, either on Buckie's coach, in the old van or thumbing it. We were young and hard working kids. The harder we worked, the more money we got and the more money we spent. On the occasions we were hitching a lift to Wigan, all we were concerned about was getting there around midnight. How we would get home didn't enter the equation, but in fairness the latest I ever got back to the Hemel turnoff was around 11.30 on the Sunday night. Although we were totally knackered we always managed to get to work or college on the Monday mornings.

We had heard stories where some of the younger lads such as Pete Wickham and Pete Townsend wouldn't arrive back until the Tuesday or the Wednesday, and once little Johnny Frazer didn't come home for a couple of weeks. But that's youth for you. They didn't need to earn as much as Yogi or me, as we were spending money right, left and centre on records and clothes.

On one particular occasion, Yogi said, "How do you fancy leaving for Wigan on Friday night after work? We can stay round Nanny Wear's house, take a look around the shops and make our way to the casino after the football."

"Okay mate, I'll be ready at 6.30 on the dot. How much are you taking to spend?"

"About a oner, (£100)" Yogi replied.

"Okay mate, I'll take the same."

On the Friday, Yogi came round in the van and off we set. There was quite a lot of traffic but we did all right and arrived in Hulme, Manchester where Yogi's Nan lived around ten o'clock, had a quick pint of beer with Uncle John, and then got our heads down for a good night's sleep. We were going to the all-nighter on the Saturday and also wanted an early start in the morning to suss out the Mancunian clothes shops. What I liked most about Manchester was the way the trendy shops were set up. It wasn't like shopping in Oxford Street, London, where all the shops were in a line each side of the road. In Manchester they were situated in blocks and under a covered roof similar to the Bullring in Birmingham. It was a lot more comfortable shopping in these new shopping precincts especially if it was raining outside, and it was in one of these places that Yogi and I found a brilliant shop called Stolen from Ivors. In this shop they sold blood-red and ice-blue Sta-Prest strides. The colours were for the United and City fans, but as I was a Liverpool fan the blood-red Sta-Prest did me just fine. I found a pair of small 28-inch waisters, took them to the changing room, tried them and asked Yogi what he thought.

Asking his opinion was as much use as a chocolate fireguard, he replied, "Well they fit all right around the waist, our kid, but you're going to have to cut about two foot off the length. The trouble with you is you've got duck's disease."

"What's that?"

"Your arse is too close to the ground, matey!"

"Yeah, I know what you mean, that's why I normally buy tailor-made but I'll give you that one, that was funny."

In the same shop, they also sold shirt jackets in a pale Ben Sherman check, which we both purchased, as we knew no one could get such clothes in London. We then found a flea market similar to the one in Kensington called the Oasis. It had an upstairs which sold new items and a downstairs that sold second-hand gear. Upstairs they sold Karmen cords, this was a thin corduroy pattern in a baggy trouser with a two and half-inch waistband (more money spent...) Whilst I was trying on the cords, a magic sound came to my ears. Just across the way, a small record stall was playing 'Daylight Saving Time' by Keith, which at the time was a Wigan gem. They also had a copy of 'Hung Up On

Your Love' by The Montclairs. I bought them both in the new decimal money—they were 60p a copy.

That night, Yogi and I went to Wigan, totally skint, but we felt that we did look the part in our new clothes. On our arrival at 'the Casino' it seemed to feel just like the early days—just the two of us. It was instant nostalgia but we knew this feeling wouldn't last long: 'STOP PUSH-ING AT THE BACK'.

The Hemel contingent would be arriving in a short while. The year was 1975 and I suppose on an average Saturday night if Jon Buck wasn't running his coach there would be about ten or fifteen of us travelling from Hemel Hempstead. The Hemel dancers' area in Wigan Casino, if you were standing at the back of the dance floor looking at the stage, was about a third of the floor towards the stage on the right hand side, that's where we used to dump our sports holdalls and mark our spot.

This particular night, Yogi reminded me that it was my twenty-first birthday in a couple of months' time—the 23rd April (Saint George's Day); a great day to have your birthday on if you're an Englishman. Yogi asked me, "What do you want for your birthday Reg?"

With no hesitation, I replied, "A copy of Dena Barnes' 'If You Ever Walk Out Of My Life' wouldn't go a miss, mate."

Yogi replied, "Yeah right, that's gonna be easy isn't it? You've got as much chance as me going to watch United as getting that sound."

"Well, you asked me what I wanted," I said.

"Think of something easier which isn't gold dust," Yogi said. "Something around a fiver and I'll see what I can do."

Back in Hemel, I asked my mum about having a birthday party and she said, "I don't see why not." So I strolled over to the Bennetts End Community Centre and hired the hall. The floor wasn't sprung loaded like 'the Casino' but at least it was wooden. Then I spoke to mum about the cake, as she made brilliant cakes.

"What would you like on it son?" Mum asked.

"Well," I said, "I want it three tiered. On the bottom, I would like Liverpool Football Club with footballers playing on a green pitch. On the second tier, the words Wigan Casino with small records stuck in the icing all round it. On top, I want me hitching a lift to Wigan holding a soul bag wearing my green cords, red short-sleeved shirt with a green soul patch on the shirt."

"You don't want much do you son! That's gonna be as hard as that bloody record you've asked Yogi to get for you."

I gave mum the same reply as I gave Yogi, "Well you asked me what I wanted."

The next thing I had to do was sort out the disco and the invitations. The disco came courtesy of Bennetts End Youth Club, and Dave Collins offered to play the records. Dave was the DJ at the youth club, so he had been playing the sounds we liked for quite some time and I knew he wouldn't play any chart stuff. I sent out about eighty invites to family and local friends who I'd grown up with, then all of the Hemel Soulies that went to Wigan. Next was some of the Caister soul crew from the weekenders, our friends from the soul clubs in London and the girls we met on holiday, who travelled down from Derby and Blackburn, and that was it.

On the night of the party, the soul music went right across the board and the floor was packed. Whatever soul music you were into, at sometime in the evening you heard what you wanted. The highlight of the night was the cake mum had made, exactly as requested.

At about nine thirty, I saw Jon Buck, Pete Wickham and Yogi on the stage. Yogi was on the mike and he called me up onto the stage. As I walked past him Yogi whispered, "Sorry mate, we couldn't get hold of Dena Barnes, so we got you 'Love You Baby' by Eddie Parker, hope that's alright."

I thought to myself, "Wow, another gem for my collection. Brilliant." I undid the wrapping and slipped the record out of its cardboard sleeve, but it wasn't a white and green Ashford label, it was a white Inferno with the words 'If You Ever Walk Out Of My Life'—Dena Barnes. I was gobsmacked.

A few weeks later, back at the Casino, I found out that quite a few Soulies from Hemel and Newbury helped pay for it. I also had great pleasure crossing it off my wants list. Later that night, I got talking to a young northern lass on the balcony who asked, "What's your favourite sound mate?"

"'If You Ever Walk Out Of My Life' by Dena Barnes. I love it," I replied.

"You've got no chance of getting that sound, there's not many people own that record. Most of the top DJs have got it and I heard a little lad in Hertfordshire has a copy."

I was so knocked out by her knowledge of who's got what, I put my arm around her shoulder and said, "And I'm not going to get a copy, am I?"

The last words she said to me were, "No chance!"

Chapter 15

Soul Searching Takes A New Direction

Shortly after my twenty-first birthday, Yogi started going out with Lorraine Hutt on a more permanent basis. So on the weekends when we were hitching to Wigan, I teamed up with little Pete Townsend. There was no way I was going to thumb any more lifts on my own after the Cleethorpes' experience. Going souling with little Pete was quite an eye opener. He was about five or six years younger than me, full of life, energy and had a superb ear for the music and for such a young lad Pete had varying taste in soul music. It wasn't just the Northern scene he was interested in; Pete also loved to play some of the other sounds in my collection especially the tunes from the Californian ballroom days, whether they were slowies or an up tempo beat, he didn't mind. He was turning out to be a true connoisseur of soul music.

Around this time of life, the summer of 1975, in our opinion the DJs were playing some of the best music we had ever heard. It appeared the music was crossing over between the Blackpool Mecca, Yate, Bristol and Wigan Casino—the sounds were slightly funkier than the earlier records, songs like: 'Name It You've Got It' by Micky Moonshine; 'Are You Ready For This?' by The Brothers; 'I Want To Give You Tomorrow' by Benny Troy; and 'Overture' by The Miracles.

Instead of three or four dudes jamming in skiffle-type bands, it was full-blown orchestras pounding out the sounds. Another good record at this time was 'Lady, Lady, Lady' by The Boogie Man Orchestra. Also some more commercial-type tunes such as 'I Love Music' by The O'Jays found itself being played within the Wigan Casino walls. It was round about this time Pete and I started to defect a bit from Wigan and we went more and more to the Bristol Intercity Soul Club, held at the Beacon in Yate. The main DJ was a tall guy they called Kojak, as he was totally bald (like me nowadays). It was at this soul club where some bastard nicked my wonderful sheepskin coat, which I was well pissed off about. I suppose these things happen now and then though.

Pete and I were also going to the all-dayers held at the Bournemouth Village Bowl venue and the Oakdale youth centre. It was at the Oakdale youth centre where I met a lovely young lady called Elaine Shepherd, who became my girlfriend for about six months, but like most relationships in the Northern soul scene where we had to travel so far it eventually fizzled out. Pete and I had some great times whilst I was going out with Elaine, as she was the sister of 'Soul Shep' who was a Golden Torch Soulie and when we stayed at Elaine's mum and dad's house, Steve (Soul Shep) used to let Pete and me play his records. The sounds Steve had were the tunes I must have missed, through not being able to get to the Torch in time before it shut down.

On one particular weekend, I left some of Steve's records that I had been playing on his mum's sideboard. But instead of telling me off for not putting them back in his record box, he said, "Those records you left on the sideboard, put them in your record box, you can have them, they are yours, call it a pressie. The only condition is that you look after them."

I am pleased to say they are still in my collection to this day.

The all-dayers held at the Village Bowl were a mix of soul music with a touch of jazz funk, which made the day more interesting. The music went right across the board, just like it did at my birthday party. It was at a soul evening held at the Village Bowl where Soul Shep dedicated a record to me: "That was the brilliant sound of 'Time Will Pass You By' by Tobi Legend. I'd like to dedicate my next sound to my little mate Reg, all the way from London. He must be the best soul fan I've ever met in my life anywhere, so especially for you Reg, is the sound of Dena Barnes' 'If You Ever Walk Out Of My Life'."

What a brilliant accolade he gave me! I still have the old tape cassette with his dedication on. The tape was a present from a friend of mine called Roland who lived in Reading. Roland just happened to have his tape recording during that evening. A few weeks later, back at the Casino, just before the third anniversary, I was having a brilliant night. I danced till about six o'clock in the morning then went and sat on the balcony. I had a good look around this magnificent place and tried to get a fixed picture in my mind. I looked over the edge of the balcony to where my lifelong friends Yogi and Lorraine were dancing beside each other and I thought to myself, 'I would particularly miss these two friends, as I have done an awful lot of souling with Yogi and I have known Lorraine since she was about six years old.' Little Pete was teaching his younger brothers about the soul scene, just as Yogi and I had shown him. Pete Wickham and John Frazer were dancing with Jethro, Sammy and the rest of the Wolverhampton crew. Debbie from Huddersfield, the girl I adored, was dancing with her friends Cheryl and Liz. Sue, Steve and Gill from Gwent, along with the rest of the Welshies, were dancing in the middle of the Casino floor. Jon Buck was right down at the front by the stage in his bid to become an important part of the Northern Soul scene.

But I felt I needed something different.

It was then that I made my decision.

So, when the night was over, I announced to everyone that I wasn't going to be going to Wigan Casino anymore, and just disappeared from the Northern soul scene.

FAVOURITE RECORDS AT THIS TIME

Salsoul Hustle	Salsoul Orchestra
Mind Blowing Decisions	Heatwave
The Chicago Theme	Hubert Laws
Party Freaks	Miami with Robert More
In The Mood	Glenn Miller
Could Heaven Ever Be Like This?	Idris Muhammad
Spanish Hustle	Fatback Band
Young Hearts Run Free	Candi Staton
Check Mate	Barrabas
Sting	Barry Waite
Waterbed	Herbie Mann
Chattanooga Choo Choo	Glenn Miller
Papaya	Ursula Dudziak
I Found Lovin	Steve Walsh
Ain't No Stopping Us Now	Mcfadden and Whitehead
Just Can't Give You Up	Mystic Merlin
I Don't Think That Man Should Sleep Alone	Ray Parker
Teardrops	Womack & Womack
Love Town	Booker Newbury III
I'll Be Around	The Spinners

Chapter 16

Dancing with Tom

Back in Hemel Hempstead, I started going to the Scamps nightclub. This was the venue that used to be called Stripes in my early clubbing days. Scamps had appeared to hit a new lease of life, especially on Monday nights. Jazz Funk Soulies from all over London were travelling into Hemel on Monday nights in search of their type of soul music. This is where I met one of the best dancers I have ever seen, his name was Tom—I never knew his second name.

Once when I asked him what he did for a living, Tom replied, "Nothing special, but I do want to be a dancer Reg."

I said, "Oh come on Tom, you're just an old street dancer; you know naff all about ballet or fine posture. You probably break all the rules of a professional dancer already. Anyway, you are too old son."

The banter was all in good fun and if ever anyone wanted Tom to make it, it was me, I really thought he was that good. Also at Scamps I met up with three marvellous girls; Jane Young, Ange Conlon and Barbara Wade. Southern Soulies at their best. The guys in their little crew were called Peter Charles (Charlie), Neville Hyde, Colin Hudson and Steve Gapp (Tigg). During the day their clothes consisted of smart bib-and-brace type jeans, cap sleeve tee shirts, kicker boots or plastic sandals. We acquired the plastic sandals from a local sub-aqua diving shop in St. Albans. In fact, we shopped most of the time in St. Albans, as this was where the best clothes shops were in and around the Hemel area. My favourite shop was called David Copperfield and to this day it is still there.

On the nights when we were going out, the crew looked like the Mafia—Gatsby style hats, coats and macs, dead smart tailor-made dresses, strides and classy Italian shoes. None of the crew minded taking out a little Northern Soul fan. It was so strange at first ditching my baggy Karman cords and my Wigan vest for a pair of 'pleated' fifties-style trousers and a mohair pullover, but that's what I did and they took me everywhere. Most of the time we headed towards London; our favourite clubs were Che Guevara, 100 Club, Watersplash in London Colney and the Cherry Trees in Welwyn Garden City. But one of the best clubs they took me to ever, was the Goldmine in Canvey Island. The top DJ was Chris Hill, he was crazy. He would play sounds such as: 'Chicago Theme' by Hubert Laws; 'Checkmate' by Barrabas; 'Sting' by Barry Waite; and 'Water Bed' Herbie Mann.

Then all of a sudden right in the middle of playing some top class jazz funk music, he threw in a Glen Miller wartime tune. Immediately all the soul fans started jiving. It was brilliant, and being dance orientated, the girls took no time at all to teach me. After all these years, I still have my infamous Goldmine badge.

One particular night there was a small soul event held at the Campus West in Welwyn Garden City. The whole crew went, as there was a dance competition. I suppose there were about thirty dancers on the floor. The DJ was Greg Edwards who nowadays is one of the top jocks on Jazz FM. He played three records then announced the winners. First was Tom, he was absolutely brilliant, second was Charlie and third was me. I felt a great sense of achievement as I had only been going around with the Jazz Funkers for about a year and to be in a competition dancing alongside Tom and Charlie was the icing on the cake.

On the Bank Holidays, we were either at Bournemouth or Margate. When we were at Margate it was as if I had travelled back in time, as the Bali Hi was still there. It was still a great place to go to, but as the venue had quite a small dance floor, we would start the evening off there until about nine o'clock, then we would head for a larger venue called the Galleon. It didn't matter what time of day it was, if there was soul music playing in the Galleon, Tom would be the centre of attention dancing in the middle of the floor. I would get a small wink or wave of acknowledgement as he carried on dancing, surrounded by Soulies admiring his dance skills. If I can remember rightly, on his feet he used to wear a black type of ballet shoe but to be honest I reckon he would have danced just as well in his bare feet.

On the afternoon of the Bank Holiday Mondays, when all the Soulies started to make their way home, word would go around of a soul do on the Isle of Sheppey. So along with the rest of the hard core Soulies, we would make our way to the Island hotel in Leys Down, which finished around midnight. Our excuse was that we went there to let the traffic die down, but really it was because we didn't want our brilliant weekends to finish.

On the Bank Holidays that we went to Bournemouth, the venues we visited mostly were the Rooftops, the Village Bowl and Pandora's in Boscombe. The larger venue was the Village Bowl; quite a few top London DJs played there. As Scamps was doing so well on Monday nights in Hemel Hempstead, when you were in the Bowl you knew so many people, as at least thirty to forty friends from the Hemel area would travel to Bournemouth on the bank holidays.

The Rooftops disco was mostly visited on the Friday night (day of arrival); as soon as you had booked in at your bed and breakfast and had a quick shower, then off you went to the Rooftops disco. It was a sort of a meeting place. Soulies from all over London and the outer regions would meet at the Rooftops. Another popular meeting place was a Long Bar called the Buccaneer near the sea front. The nightclub called Pandora's was just out of town in Boscombe. Pandora's was quite a small nightclub; the type of place where you could take the girl who you had met the previous night in the Village Bowl out for a change of scenery.

Although I had left Wigan Casino, I was still attending Northern Soul do's in the South such as the Beacon in Bristol, selective nights at Pandora's in Boscombe, the Point in Southampton and the 100 Club in London.

It was at the Beacon in Bristol where I met a girl called Janie from Malvern in Worcester—we went out with each other for quite a while. Janie had a bed-sit in Bournemouth, which was quite handy for us as Janie and I liked to shop for retro clothing in the second hand shops in and around the Boscombe area. When we weren't staying in Bournemouth, we would stay at my mum's house back in Hemel Hempstead. Janie quickly became friends with Ange, Jane and Barbs who welcomed her with open arms. So now, when we went out altogether, we had another Northern Soul fan enjoying the Jazz Funk scene as much as I did.

It was when I was out with Janie at a small Northern Soul club in Camberley that I purchased my Poppies LP. At the time, I paid fifteen pounds for it. I bought the LP for the track 'The Love We Knew', (later to be called 'Pain In My Heart'). After playing the rest of the tracks on the LP, I was well pleased with my purchase and felt it was well worth the sum of fifteen pounds.

My relationship with Janie eventually came to an end. It wasn't due to the miles I was travelling this time, it was because Janie was overdoing it with the Jack & Jills (amphetamines). I worshipped the ground she walked on, but when she got into a situation where she couldn't afford to pay her rent, I suggested that she went back to her Dad's house in Malvern (Worcester).

During the following week I had a letter from Janie saying that she had made up with her dad and promised that she would get herself sorted out.

The letter ended with, "Who knows, I might bump into you one day." So that was the end of that.

FAVOURITE RECORDS AT THIS TIME

Pillow Talk	Lou Donaldson
Mr Bojangles	Nina Simone
The Way We Were	Willis Jackson
Let's Straighten It Out	Latimore
Flight Time	Donald Byrd
Time After Time	Miles Davis
Daylight	Bobby Womack
You Make Me Feel Brand New	Jimmy Castor-Bunch
Place And Spaces/Dominoes	Donald Byrd
Walking In Rhythm	Blackbirds
Got To Be With You Tonight	Bobbie Womack
Human Nature	Miles Davis
Reaching Out For Your Love	Tamiko Jones
Mercy Mercy Me	Grover Washington Jr
Morning Dance	Spyro Gyro
Inner City Blues	Grover Washington Jr
Until You Come Back To Me	Hill Street Soul

Chapter 17

In Search Of Where My Music Was Taking Me

I was going souling on quite a frequent basis with the Hemel Jazz Funk crew, and after a few months of going to the Goldmine in Canvey Island and all the other places mentioned in the previous chapter, little Ange announced that it was her birthday in a couple of weeks' time, and she would like to celebrate it at Ronnie Scott's Jazz Club. So we hired a twelve-seater mini bus and off we went to Frith Street in London.

Opposite Ronnie Scott's were a few Italian coffee bars which instantly reminded me of the stories from the old mod days where they would meet in the espresso coffee bars before going on to the old jazz clubs such as the Flamingo or the Scene Club. The only things missing were the scooters; if there were a couple parked outside one of the coffee bars, it would have felt like instant nostalgia.

Inside Ronnie Scott's there was a fantastic atmosphere. If I can remember rightly, there was dim red and blue lighting and a smallish stage, but on this stage they had massive artists such as Hubert Laws, Donald Bird, Miles Davis and many others.

'In Search Of Where My Music Was Taking Me'—seeing live jazz acts, I felt I'd reached the summit. It was quite strange that in the early Wigan days, vocals were added to brilliant up-tempo instrumentals. Yet in the jazz clubs, some of the songs we already knew the vocals to, were being played by such exceptional musicians that it seemed they made their instruments sound like they were saying the words. Typical examples of this work would be the likes of: 'Mercy, Mercy, Me' by Grover

Washington Jr; 'The Way We Were' by Willis Jackson; 'Human Nature' by Miles Davis; and 'Pillow Talk' by Lou Donaldson.

And let's not forget the brilliant version of 'Time After Time' by Miles Davis—music of the highest quality in my opinion. This instrumental, alongside 'What's Going On?' by The Funk Brothers, has to be the best I have ever heard.

After spending some time hitting the jazz clubs, I had to create some more space in my record box for this type of music. At this time I was purchasing sounds such as: 'Mr Bojangles' by Nina Simone; 'Let's Straighten It Out' by Latimore; 'Reaching Out For Your Love' by Tamiko Jones; and another favourite has to be 'Until You Come Back To Me' by Hill Street Soul.

I don't think many of us Soulies realised at the time just how powerful our music was, and how it was going to set out our lives in the way it did. Millions of us out there had the same thing in common, friendships of the highest order. Even though we all came from different walks of life, our connection with each other was through our soul, and long may it continue even in the afterlife.

In my dream, we're all dancing on our clouds upstairs, with sprung loaded maple dance floors, floating to our all time favourite sounds. Now that would be a perfect way to finish up, wouldn't it?

Anyway, these are only my treasured thoughts, so before you all think I'm away with the mixer, I'll get back to the jazz clubs. The music in the jazz clubs had to be the most professional music I had ever heard. I often wondered if the early Modernists/Mods felt the same impact that I had, the music just blew me away especially as some of the jazz artists recorded a few of the Soul Dance Classics like 'Time Is Tight' by Booker T and The MGs; 'Wade In The Water' by Ramsey Lewis; and 'Sliced Tomatoes' by The Just Brothers.

Through the next few years I kept Souling but it was mostly on my own because as you get older, most ordinary people get married. All the little crews I had been a part of were disappearing as my friends entered the lifestyles of the normal, but I was only twenty-four and far too young for that kind of caper.

In 1977/78 a ski centre was built in Hemel Hempstead. Skiing was something I was interested in as a small kid, so I trained and learned the finer aspects of skiing and finally became a ski instructor. All of my ski friends knew about my records but it was only every now and then that we would get them out and give them a spin. At the time, if I ever went souling it was because I was asked to take people who hadn't been before. I remember on one occasion the manager of the ski centre, Roy Surrey, took about twenty of us out for a Christmas celebration at Baileys nightclub in Watford, which used to be known as the Top Rank. On the night that Roy booked, it happened to be when Tommy Hunt was appearing. Dave Surrey, a friend called Martin Thurnham and I volunteered to get the drinks with the kitty while the rest of the party sat at tables right by the stage. Whilst the three of us were waiting to get served Tommy Hunt announced that a Northern Soul dancer was going to dance for the audience.

I said to Martin who was the tallest of us, "Hurry up mate, I'm bound to know the Northern Soul dancer."

Once Martin had been served, we made a quick dash to the tables. All three of us had a tray of drinks each and when we reached where we were sitting, Tommy said, "We'll give the lad time to put his tray of drinks down and he will come up on the stage and dance for us."

It was then I realised the guy Tommy was talking about was me. It was obvious that one of the party had set me up big time, so as much as I was looking for a different type of soul music, it felt that I was kept being called back to the Northern Soul scene on various occasions.

Chapter 18

Life Takes A Massive U-Turn

During the course of the next twenty years, life changed dramatically. I lost touch with Yogi for a while as he left Hemel Hempstead to work at a holiday camp and became a Blue Coat. Then within two years, he had worked his way up the ladder to become Entertainments Manager. I remember when we were kids he told me that one day he would like to hire top class soul acts. Yogi achieved that dream when one day, he hired The Drifters as the cabaret for one of his night-spots. So like me, Yogi was still keeping in touch with his soul and still doing little bits and pieces.

One of my old friends, Sue Hussey, who worked in our local Woolworths, asked me if I would take her and some of her mates away for the weekend, so I took them to Margate. There were about six of us; me, Sue Hussey, Karen Hussey, Shirley Holland, Elizabeth Curl (Curley) and Bev Morris.

Five girls and one geezer—I didn't stand a flipping chance. Why does the female species take three hours to get ready? By the time I got a bath, the water was always cold. Also, they nicked some of my cardigans, every time I looked for my designer ski cardi, which my Granny Stickings had made me, Shirley Holland would be wearing it.

We spent most of the time in the Bali Hi and to be fair to the girls, they weren't all that bad. The music was top drawer and the girls were excellent company, so what more could a man ask for? The funniest girl in the crew was Bev Morris; the one-liners she would come out with were second to none and had us all in stitches every minute of the weekend. But the big man upstairs works in mysterious ways and about five months later our Bev passed away after being diagnosed with a brain haemorrhage due to bumping her head in the back garden. It's times like this I look up into the sky and think 'What's the point? Why do you always take the best?' Apart from my sister Jackie who most of the time is away with the mixer, young Bev Morris was the funniest person I had ever met.

"God Bless You Soul Sister, I'll see you when I get there."

As I said, I was still doing little bits and pieces in the Soul music world and one of the best nights I had was something out of nothing really. Ange Conlon's little sister Elaine, asked if I was free one Saturday.

"Why, what did you have in mind, sister?" I said.

She replied, "Will you take me to Baileys night club in Watford?"

"Of course I will, just let me know when you want to go."

On the Saturday night when I took Elaine there was supposed to be just a resident band playing, but before they were due on stage the compere announced that two disco dancers were going to perform instead. Elaine and I were sitting at a table near the stage, the lights went down and two guys waddled onto the stage dressed as Laurel and Hardy; both were carrying a bent cane and wearing the traditional bowler hat. On each side of the stage, was an old-fashioned hat and coat stand. Both dancers were doing some clumsy dance steps and then in sequence hung their wooden canes on the stands, flipped off their bowler hats, which ran down their right arms into their hands, and placed them on the hat stands, then they ripped off their jackets and started to dance. One of the dancers was oriental; both were wearing shiny satin tops and were such exceptional dancers the audience were clapping every move. After about ten minutes and two records later, I took a closer look at the dancer nearest our table. He looked straight at me, winked and gave me a quick wave of acknowledgement.

I said to Elaine, "Oh my God, it's Tom, I can't believe it—he's made it."

I could hardly contain myself. The show lasted for about three quarters of an hour and all I kept thinking was, 'Wow, he's made it'. I was chatting with Elaine when an official type bloke called us over to the stage door where Tom was waiting, then with a firm handshake and a head to head hug, I said, "Well done, Tom."

He replied, "You were right Reg, it took ages to master the posture and the ballet steps, but I got there in the end. I'm booked up for three stage shows in London, then I will see how it goes, but how ever long it lasts I'm just going to enjoy life for the moment."

Well done Tom!

At the age of twenty-seven, I started to follow the norm. I met a girl called Debbie in the most unusual circumstances. It all happened one Friday night. At the time I was sub-contracting for a local building company, Borras Construction, when the foreman insisted we worked late to finish a certain job. This situation did not go down well with yours truly—it's a Friday night, soul music being played by the bucket load at the Queen's Head public house in our local town and where am I? Working in the middle of London.

By the time I finally arrived back at home where I lived with my Mum and Dad, it was ten fifteen. This was far too late to get washed, changed and head off down the Queen's Head (last orders were at quarter to eleven in those days).

As I walked through the front door of my house, my Mum said, "Where have you been? All your mates said they would meet you down at the Queen's Head."

"I know Mum but it's far too late now. Who was with Steve Surrey?"

"Jane Hill and Alison Temple."

"Oh not Alison. That's really made me happy now, ain't it. Oh sod it! I'm going over the Cockerel. I'll be back just after eleven."

"You can't go out like that Son; you look like a little gypsy."

"That'll be all right Mum. At least if I meet a nice girl she'll know that I'm a grafter and not a lazy so-and-so."

I must admit I did look scruffy and covered in dust but not to go out on a Friday night would have been sacrilege. So I swiftly walked over to the Golden Cockerel, the nearest pub to where I lived. On arrival, I purchased a lager top. Instead of mingling around, like I normally do when I'm out, I kept a low profile standing by the bar. The thoughts running through my mind were of Steve and the two girls down the Queen's. If I'd been out with them I would have probably been on my fifth snakebite by now (Old English cider and lager—a lethal concoction that went cloudy when the two drinks were mixed).

My thoughts were drifting away when I noticed Debbie Brooks—a young lady I'd admired when I was younger. She appeared to be heading towards the ladies' loo. I was just about to tap her on the shoulder when I thought, "Hang on you idiot. You're gonna have to use every tactic in the book to chat her up. Look at yourself fresh from the scaffold and looking like shit—you've nearly blown it! Rule number one: don't try to chat up a bird when she's heading for the loo. You won't have time to sell yourself because she's dying to use the loo. Wait till the lady in question returns, then try and stop her in her stride."

On this occasion, my dress code was going to do nothing for me, so I had to rely on my personality and wit. As Debbie was about to walk past where I was standing, I tapped her on the shoulder and said, "Hello Sue, how are you?"

"My name's not Sue. Try again."

"Is it Sheila?" Debbie shook her head and said, "No it isn't."

"I'm only havin' you on," I said. "Of course I know who you are. You're Debbie Brooks. I loved you when we were kids, then you went and got married."

"I've got news for you Reg. I'm not any more."

"You're not? I'm sorry Deb, what went wrong there then?"

"I was far too young. I'm afraid I let my heart rule my head."

"I wouldn't worry Deb, these things happen. Sorry I look so scruffy, I called in the pub straight from work."

"Hey, I don't look so good myself Reg, marriage break-ups take their toll!"

"Last orders at the bar," cried the landlady.

"Can I get you a drink Debbie?"

"Well, I'm with a friend, Diane."

"Go and ask her what she wants while I get served." Five minutes later, this scruffy little urchin is chatting up two tasty looking women. In our conversation, I asked Debbie if she was getting out much.

"Not really," Deb replied, "I seem to have lost a bit of confidence out there."

"No, you haven't. You'll be all right. Would you like to come out with me tomorrow? I'm going to the CB club for a drink. You're welcome to come with me if you want to."

"You're in a CB club?" Debbie laughed, "what, 'ten four good buddy' and all that jazz? Have you got a secret call sign?"

"If you stop laughing, I'll tell you. For a start it's not called a 'call sign', it's called a handle, and on the airwaves I'm called India November Charlie Hotel (INCH)."

"Inch!" Debbie replied, as the two girls were falling about laughing their heads off. "Why Inch? Is it because...?"

"No it isn't! It's because of my height, and when I'm at work I refuse to change to metric."

Then the landlady called 'time'. As we were filtering out of the door of the pub, Diane said to Debbie, "If I was you, I'd go out with Reg tomorrow. I've never seen you laugh like that—you'll have a great time."

Debbie said, "Give us a ring around six and I'll see how I feel."

The very next day I was working for Steve Surrey's mum, Audrey. I was doing a little job for her in her kitchen when Steve appeared with his hands holding his head asking his mother "Have you got a couple of aspirins Mum? My head's splitting! Can't you use that hammer quietly, Reg?"

I smiled at Steve and replied, "That's what you get for drinking those snakebites, Son."

"Yeah, all right mate. Anyway, what happened to you last night?"

"I had a quiet night really Steve. I got home from work late and with only half hour's drinking time left I strolls over the Cockerel. Chatted up a really nice bird and I might be seeing her tonight."

"No you didn't. Tell him, Mum. Reg reckons he's met a gorgeous bird up the Cockerel."

"If that's what Reg says, why should you doubt him?"

"Because, Mother, when we're out, I do all the talking."

"Exactly," replied Audrey, "and what results has he had with you?" Whilst all three of us were laughing, I asked Steve what his plans were for the Saturday evening.

Steve replied, "We're all going to Cesar's Palace in Luton. We're meeting up the Plough in Leverstock Green around eight o'clock."

"Okay then Steve. If I walk in the Plough at eight with my new girlfriend hanging on me arm, you buy my drink and whatever Debbie wants. Is that a deal?"

"And what if you don't?" replied Steve.

"If I don't, I will buy you two pints of snakebite down the Queen's Head next Friday."

Steve slapped my right hand with his and said, "It's a deal."

Then I packed up my tools and said to Steve, "I'll see you later mate."

"Yeah, we'll see," replied Steve rubbing his hands together.

Around about five thirty that Saturday afternoon I phoned Debbie and arranged to pick her up at 7.30pm.

Right on time, I rang the bell and Debbie's dad Cyril opened the front door of their house.

"Hello Son, I haven't seen you since you and Debbie were teenagers. Where are you taking her then?"

"Only to the CB club Cyril. I'll have her home by eleven-thirty."

Debbie's Dad laughed and said, "That rule doesn't apply anymore Reg. She's twenty-four now, she can come and go when she pleases."

At that point Debbie appeared from behind her Dad. "Okay Reg, I'm ready."

"We've got to go to the Plough first," I quickly said, "One of my customers owes me some money." I was holding Debbie's hand as I walked through the door of the pub then I heard Steve say to Al and Jane,

"Oh no! Excuse me girls, I've got to buy Reg and his girlfriend some drinks."

He strolled over and I said, "All right Steve? This is my friend Debbie."

Steve held Debbie's hand, kissed her on the side of her cheek and said, "What would you like to drink?"

Debbie replied, "A vodka and orange squash."

"And mine's a lager top please Steve."

Whilst Debbie was talking to Jane and Alison I said, "This is a lovely pint of lager top, mate."

Steve replied, "I expect it is you little shit! I'll win it back one day."

I started seeing Debbie on a regular basis and she soon became a part of our little crew which consisted of Steve, Jane, Alison, Colin French, Debbie and myself. The pubs we mostly used were the White Horse in Leverstock Green, and for the music it was always the Queen's Head near Hemel town. To help Debbie get back on her feet, restore her confidence and put some money in her pocket, another friend, Kenny Bateman, and I started to take Debbie to work with us on Saturdays. Although Kenny and I were sub-contracting for Borras, if Debbie helped us on Saturdays we would give her some wages out of our own pockets. We taught her how to build studwork partitions, plaster board ceilings and fit skirting. There was one time we even taught her how to hang a door. All this was to become a great learning curve for Debbie as at the time she had no idea that one day we would be building a house together.

After about two years of seeing each other, I managed to get a mortgage on a small cottage that needed quite a bit of restoration work. When the cottage was at its worst, it looked like a lift shaft. There were just four walls; whilst standing in the front room if you looked up between the roof timbers you could see the sky. In fact the roof timbers were made from split logs so, as that was the only timber we managed to salvage in the whole house, we called our home "Split Logs Cottage". Eventually Debbie and I got married and the record we picked for our wedding dance was George Benson's version of "Unchained Melody".

Although Debbie doesn't like my music much and doesn't attend many of the soul do's that I go too, she is the main strength behind the little man on the dance floor. My wife's idea of paradise is me out on a Saturday night, while she is watching her favourite television programmes munching on a box of Milk Tray chocolates. On a normal Saturday night, the clothes I have chosen to wear would be washed, ironed and laid out in our bedroom all ready for me after having a bath.

So the 'choon' I would like to dedicate to my lovely wife Debbie, is "Give Your Baby A Standing Ovation" by The Dells.

The record in question is a live recording. It starts with a load of clapping and cheering by the audience, then one of the Dells says something like: "Although we're the stars of the show, behind every star, as behind every great man there is, there is a woman, and if you're a man who's got a woman, I think that we should take a little time to salute this woman and give this woman a great big round of applause."

My wife deserves more than a round of applause, she deserves a bloody medal. So, as I've said, although Debbie isn't keen on my music, she is behind her little man one hundred and fifty percent. If I am waiting for an exclusive piece of vinyl through the post, on its arrival Debbie will ring me at work to let me know it is here. Also if I'm going away for a soul weekender, Debbie will start gathering bits and pieces that she thinks I am going to need in the week previous to the event.

So as the record by Ike Strong says, "I Owe My Life To You!!!"

I was still souling but on a very small scale. One of the office staff at the local timber merchants called Ian Hopla, who was a regular Caister boy, would now and then get tickets for Soul concerts. With Ian I saw Barry White at the Royal Albert Hall and Bill Withers at the Hammersmith Odeon. Then my accountant, Kate Watts who was also a ski companion of mine took me to see Alexander O'Neal at Wembley. As time went on, I saw Shakatak at the Knebworth Jazz Festival. When they had finished their act, they stood next to Debbie and me alongside our friends, Jane Hill and Steve Surrey, whilst we all watched the Crusaders. It was quite strange really when a classy group like Shakatak were blown away as much as we were by the performance of Randy Crawford and the rest of the Crusaders.

There was also one weekend when Debbie went away with some of the girls. A young lad called Adam Bisney (Biz) knocked at my front door. I knew Adam through my work cos Adam was a felt roofer and worked for a local roofing company, so I thought that he had come round for something concerning work. I asked Biz what he wanted. He said he had heard about my records and asked if he could hear some when I had a spare moment.

"Well," I said, "if you're not doing anything tonight you can pop around and we'll have a little play of them."

Whilst I was waiting for Biz to arrive, I thought, "This reminds me of the day when I only had one record and was invited to hear Terry Bartlett's collection when I was about fourteen."

Within an hour of Biz arriving, we were both tiptoeing around the front room, as the entire carpet was covered with records. We started playing at 6.30 on the Saturday and when we had finished the time was ten o'clock Sunday morning.

I looked at Biz and said "Welcome to the world of all-nighters."

When winter arrived, I went away skiing to Hintertux in Austria with Debbie and the other ski instructors from the ski centre. On the second day of our holiday, there was a whiteout, so because there wasn't much skiing going on due to the weather, my first child was conceived, a little girl. My wife and I thought it quite apt to call her Holly.

Sometime between my daughter and son being born, I managed to attend two all-nighters; the first was my old friend Jacko's funeral benefit night held at Newbury. I met John Frazer and his wife Karen at a pub called the Wagon and Horses in Hemel Hempstead and when Jon Buck and his wife Sue arrived, we all went together. One of the highlights of the evening was seeing so many old faces such as Liz and Alan from Reading and Jethro from Wolverhampton. Jethro was still dancing as well as he did when I left Wigan Casino.

The second all-nighter I went to was one of Jon Buck's RSG do's held at the Unicorn in Leighton Buzzard. It was just like the old days when I was younger. I purchased a record; it was one that had slipped my net, the sound of Velvet Satin's 'Nothing Can Compare To You'.

Two years after Holly was born, along came my son Jack, three months premature. This was when my life took a massive U-turn. After a year of looking after a premature baby, Jack caught a very rare disease called Kawasaki Syndrome. With Debbie taking endless trips to Great Ormond Street Children's Hospital and me looking after my little girl Holly, I'm afraid souling was definitely put on the back burner.

We were coping okay, but as I was a sub-contractor, I didn't like letting the governor down, so it was then that I decided to work for myself.

I built a workshop in my back garden and worked one-day on and one-day off. On the days off, Holly and I travelled to Great Ormond Street to visit Jack and Debbie. This set-up was working okay until one day I was fitting a staircase and it slipped. Like an idiot I tried to save it and 'did my back in'. I ended up on traction for seven weeks and being self-employed I got nothing from the government, my mortgage was frozen and debts started to mount up which left my wife hanging on to the house the best way she could. I am pleased to say we still live in the same house, but like most people we are just about hanging in there.

During the time I was in traction, I made a pledge with my mates that however tight it got (you know what I mean) that I wouldn't sell any of my records. I am so pleased that I didn't. It would be impossible sharing my experiences with you without the sounds.

Then came the year of my fortieth birthday. I asked Mum, "Do people celebrate their fortieth birthdays?"

Mum replied, "Of course they do Son, what kind of cake would you like this time?"

"Do you think you could make a record Mum?"

"Easy," Mum replied, "but the black icing might put your mates off eating it. What record is it going to be Son? You've got so bloody many."

"It's going to be 'Sitting On The Dock Of The Bay' by Otis Redding on a blue Stax label. That's the one I would like if possible."

The party was a huge success just like my twenty-first, the only thing different was the Soulies were a lot older, but they could still dance as good.

Without going out so often, the only access to the music was via the wireless. The artists that turned my head and emptied my pockets were performers like Luther Vandross, Shakatak, The Crusaders, Boyz2men etc, and the one artist that I still think is the best thing since sliced bread was the sound of Sade. Apart from being so gorgeous, to me Sade was a fresh new sound, which was well appreciated.

Twenty-odd years later, after building the house, getting married, starting my own business and nursing a sick child, at the age of forty-seven I had a phone call. A blast from the past, little Pete Townsend's wife Jane asked if I would like to go to Pete's fortieth birthday party. We got the DJ to play some old tunes, so we had a little dance. As the night went on and the more drinks we had I spoke to Dave, Pete's brother about hiring a hall and playing some of our old soul records. Jackie, Dave's wife, said it was the beer talking.... and it wouldn't happen.... So the next day she was pleasantly surprised when I called and off we went to hire Bennetts End Youth Club—after all those years it was still there.

We had no idea it was going to change our lives once again.

RECORDS BOUGHT AROUND THIS TIME

Happy	William Bell
Love, Love, Love	Bobby Hebb
I Have Faith In You	Edwin Starr
Be Young Be Foolish Be Happy	The Tams
Sock It To 'em JB	Rex Garvin
I Need My Baby	Jackie Beavers
Washed Ashore	The Platters
My World Is Empty Without You	Stevie Wonder
Agent Double Soul	Edwin Starr
You Don't Care Anymore	Jodie Mathis
If That's What You Want	Frank Beverley and The Butlers
Sweet Thing	The Spinners
I'll Do Anything	Doris Troy
Times A Wasting	Fuller Brothers
Just Walk In My Shoes	Gladys Knight
A Case Of Love	Sequins
One Wonderful Moment	The Shakers
Quick Change Artist	The Soul Twins
There's A Ghost In My House	R Dean Taylor
Love Is Like An Itching In My Heart	Timothy Wilson
Breakaway	Ernie Bush
I Can't Live This Way	Barnaby Bye
Time	Edwin Starr
I Ain't Going Nowhere	Jr Walker and The All Stars
This Old Heart Of Mine	Tammi Terrell
Afternoon On The Rhino	Mike Post Coalition

Chapter 19

Northern Soul is Reborn Again!

So that Dave and I could buy some DJ equipment, we drew up a list of about eighty friends who might be interested in a Northern Soul night and we sold the tickets for £5 each. Dave's brother, little Pete Townsend, knew a lad who was selling a pair of second hand record decks with a thing called a mixer, so off we went to buy them. The amp and the speakers followed with the help of some money Dave and I provided. Then Dave and I made a large box out of MDF in my workshop to mount the decks and mixer in. After that we made the disco stand. We took the stand up to Dave's house and his son Danny painted some brilliant soul cartoon characters on the front of the stand.

Dave and I phoned up two Soulies that we thought might be interested in helping us. One was Yogi, and the other was the young lad called Adam Bisney. Both said they were definitely up for it. It wasn't until the practice night before the do did we allow Yogi and Biz to see the artwork that young Danny had painted, as the characters on the stand resembled ourselves. Both Yogi and Biz were well impressed, not only by the artwork, but also by the equipment that Dave and I had managed to buy.

On the night, Dave and I had the day off work. Our day started by going to the local café for a big brekkie, then we went to Past and Present, a record shop in Watford, that was still there after thirty years and our friend Mick Boland was still working there. Mick was one of the guys Yogi and I met the first time we went to the Leeds Soul Festival. Mick was an ex-Golden Torch boy; he was the chap who advised me to buy 'Skiing In The Snow' by The Invitations. In his own words: "It's going to be big," and it was massive by the time I got to go to the Casino. Dave and I told Mick that we were running a Soul night that evening.

"Brilliant. Are you starting it all off again? I'll let any customers who I think might be interested know about it."

In Mick's shop I bought a Darrell Banks CD to play as background music whilst we were setting up the hall for our Soul night. At about four o'clock, we were allowed into the youth club. It took no time at all to set up our decks and test the equipment. Dave and I had something else up our sleeves. At Wigan Casino, down by the stage they had a couple of large ultraviolet tubes, the type that show you up when you're wearing anything white, so just like the Casino, Dave and I made a small one and hung it just in front of the disco unit. After that we added the finishing touches such as ashtrays, peanut bowls and nibble trays ready for when the girls came back from shopping.

We arranged to meet Yogi, Biz, little Pete and the girls at six thirty. When they arrived we told them to wait by the door until we were ready. We put on the Darrell Banks CD, set the lights up and shouted, "Okay you can come in now."

Well they couldn't believe it—the atmosphere was perfect, just like a little seedy jazz club. We knew that we had sold at least fifty tickets and on the door Debbie and Pete's wife Jane had another forty. They were all sold before 9.30, so the first night was a sell-out and everyone had a brilliant time.

The next day I had loads of people phone me, and one even stopped me in my car to ask when the next do was, I thought to myself, 'Oh dear, here we go again.' Although we had about two thousand records between us, we felt we needed some more, but where could we purchase vinyl nowadays?

The following week my mum and dad asked if I would like to go to Yarmouth with them. I thought it would be a good idea, mum had been pretty ill with cancer for a number of years and my sister and brother had been on a couple of holidays with them so this was my turn. Mum loved shopping for seaside tat in a road called Regent Street in Yarmouth. It was when I was walking around one of these shopping arcades that I heard some Northern Soul music being played. I spoke to the floor manager who turned out to be a chap called Andy Saggers, one of Yarmouth's top Northern Soul DJs. I asked him if he knew where I could buy vinyl these days, he gave me a DJ called Shaun Chapman's phone number. Shaun ironically only lived about ten miles from Hemel Hempstead and ran a Northern Soul night at RAF Halton called the Aylesbury Soul Club, where he sold vinyl records. It appeared to me that the music was still bubbling in small clubs all over the country and was about to erupt again, twenty-five years from where we left it.

The next do we put on had to be in a much bigger hall called Nash Mills. The Nash Mills do's were brilliant, we chose that particular venue for the floor. It doesn't have to be sprung loaded, but in our opinion if it isn't wooden it's not worth having. Through going to Shaun Chapman's Soul Club, we attracted a much bigger crowd at ours. It was great to see the likes of Shaun dancing more than selling his sounds and the only complaint he had was that he couldn't walk for about three days after the event. Shaun took the time to phone me and said it was a brilliant night—it was a back to basics evening playing for the floor and the paying public. It means so much when you get a phone call like that especially from someone like Shaun Chapman and it's nice to know that all your efforts have been appreciated.

"Thanks Shaun, We'll see you next time!"

FAVOURITE RECORDS AROUND THIS TIME

Call Me	Eddie Bishop
Stars	Barbara Lewis
If I Could Only Be Sure	Nolan Porter
Because Of You	Jackie Wilson
Whatever Happened	Eddie Holman
I'm Coming Home Baby	Mel Torme
Look Back Over Your Shoulder	Archie Bell And The Drells
Getting Mighty Crowded	Betty Everett
Big Thing	Sapphires
Home Is Where The Heart Is	Bobbie Womack
Baby Reconsider	Leon Haywood
We Got To Keep On	The Casanova Two
Let Me Be Your Boy	Wilson Pickett
Nothing Too Good For My Baby	The Springers
Do I Love You?	Frank Wilson
Magic Touch	Melba Moore
Kissing My Love Goodbye	Betty Swann
I Can't Break The News To Myself	Ben E King
I'll Be Your Champion	Jimmy Soul Clark
House For Sale	Millie Jackson
Open The Door To Your Heart	Darrell Banks
Don't Pretend	The Belles
No One To Love	Pat Lewis
My Little Girl	Bob And Earl
Love Factory	Eloise Laws
He Who Picks A Rose	Jimmy Ruffin

Chapter 20

A Scooter, At Your Age?

As things were pretty sweet at the moment, I thought I would try and pay back some of the money we owed, so I extended my mortgage, but at the age I was, I was too old to get enough to clear it. All this was a massive mistake on my behalf as the money owed was on those dreaded credit cards. As I said before, my wife was trying to hang onto the house when things out of the norm were happening. Now at the moment, credit cards are unsecured loans and if your wages don't meet the criteria, through the Citizens Advice Bureau you can have those extortionate interest rates frozen, whilst you try to pay what you can. I hope you don't mind me writing about this, but I felt it necessary as it might help someone else in the same boat. Credit cards can't take your house off you but failing to pay your rent (mortgage) can!

Anyway, after a lot of paying out, I had about four hundred quid left and I heard that a friend of mine called Paul Turvey was selling his old scooter. He asked if I knew anyone who might be interested in buying it.

I said, "I'd love to buy it myself. How old is it?"

Paul said, "It was made in 1958 Reg, it's nearly as old as you."

I replied, "It can't be that fucking old 'Topsy', what you asking for it?"

"I was going to put it in the paper for six hundred quid, but if you want it you can have it for four."

So that was it. I was now the proud owner of a 152 L2 Vintage Vespa with a 150 Super engine. I knew Dave Townsend had a 150 Super so I gave him a phone call.

"Hi Dave, I've just bought Topsy Turvey's old scooter."

"You ain't. A scooter at your age—whatever next? You've never ridden one have you?"

"No, but it looks all right,"

"They're not for bloody looking at they're for bloody riding, I'll be right down."

When Dave arrived we were both killing ourselves laughing.

"Does it work?" Dave asked.

"Of course it does, Paul dropped it off this morning." Opposite my workshop there was a small industrial estate, so Dave kicked the scooter over and gave it a whirl.

"It's all right," he said. "The steering bearings are a bit loose but nothing that can't be put right. On you get."

Dave pointed out how it works and off I went. It was a bit jumpy at first but once I got the hang of the gear change I was okay. I bloody loved it; it was so cool. I thought, 'what have I been missing all these years?' It was such a brilliant feeling riding a vintage Vespa that belonged to me. "Right, what's next, how do I get insured?"

"You can't yet," Dave replied, "you have to pass your CBT motor bike test—it's about ninety quid."

"Oh dear," I thought, "I haven't even told the missus about the motor scooter yet."

Once I told Debbie, she suggested I phone Julie Meager, a friend of the family whose boyfriend happened to run a motorbike training school. A week later I passed my CBT and the fee was only forty-five quid. A couple of weeks later I got insured and was "cookin' on full gas".

Dave suggested for our next 'Soul do' that he would put an ad in the local paper to see if he could drag up some of the old St. Albans Soulies that used to attend the all-nighters with us. He was exactly right. A few of the old faces phoned and said they would like to come to the do and asked how they get the tickets. Dave would get their addresses and we would deliver them on our scooters. Then we had a phone call from a guy called Kev Matthews, who was into scooters and ran a scooter club with some friends and asked if we would like to go. It was held at a pub called the Plough and Harrow in Harpenden, the last Wednesday of every month. The club was called the SAS (St. Albans Scooters).

The night that Dave and I went, Kev Matthews was waiting outside for us and there was about fifteen scooters parked up. Kev said that he recognised me from the Jazz/Funk days.

"I know you," he said. "You're a friend of Tom's. He's still dancing you know."

I replied, "Well he was good wasn't he?"

It wasn't until I walked into the club that I realised that the scooter scene was so closely linked to my music. There were two DJs called Ross and Dell playing a mixture of Reggae, Northern Soul and Mod Style Sounds. Kev then introduced me to another guy called Jimmy who helped run the club.

Kev said, "If you want to know anything about Northern Soul music, Jimmy speak to Reg. He was going before the Mod revival."

It was at that moment that I began to get a clearer picture of what I think must have happened. I had left the Northern Soul scene after the third Wigan anniversary, then there was the Mod revival due to the release of the film *Quadrophenia* and that's when I believe the scooters started to appear again. I swear that all the time Yogi and I were souling, I never once saw a scooter at an all-nighter. Jimmy, Ross, Dell, Peter and a few others wanted to know what it was like walking across that sprung loaded floor at Wigan or going up the escalator to the Highland Room at the Blackpool Mecca. After about fifteen minutes, there were about half a dozen scooterists listening and asking questions. I felt like Hans Christian Andersen, with a small audience showing such enthusiasm and listening to what I had to say. Later that evening I said to Jimmy that I would make him a tape of some of my records. He said loads of people have promised me that, but it's never happened.

"Don't worry Jimmy, even though we've only just met, it will this time."

The following month at the SAS club, I popped the tape in Jimmy's pocket; he was over the moon, "Reg you didn't forget, brilliant."

What he didn't know was in between 'Time Will Pass You By' by Tobi Legend and 'If You Ever Walk Out Of My Life' by Dena Barnes was the live dedication that Soul Shep had done for me all those years ago. After that, the other scooterists approached me about the music and the places we had been too.

This is when I decided to write my story and through Dave's ad in the local paper we now had a scooter club to go to, and a lot more people began to attend the Bennetts End Soul Club nights.

RECORDS BOUGHT AROUND THIS TIME

Too Late	Mandrill
Baby Don't Waste Your Time	Gladys Knight
Make Sure You Have Someone To Love You	The Dells
Ain't Got No Problems	Sunday
Sweeter Than The Day Before	The Valentinos
Blue Skies	Jackie Wilson
Lonely Girl	The Side Show
Girl I've Been Trying To Tell You	The Ultimates
Moonlight Music And You	Laura Green
Making New Friends	Gene Tracey
Girl, You're My Kind Of Wonderful	The Ultimates
Count Me Out	Billy Stewart
Talkin'	The Vee Gees
Tried And Convicted	Bobby Womack
Prayin'	Harold Melvin
Sweetest Feelin'	Irma and Jackie
My Love Is Your Love	Isley Brothers
Pour Your Little Heart Out	The Drifters
I'll Hold You	Frankie and Johnny
I Still Love You	Seven Souls
The 81	Candy And Kisses
Seven Days	Tammy Lavette
You Know How To Love Me	Phyllis Hyman
The Way You've Been Acting Lately	Al Kent

Chapter 21

Here We Go Again

As we predicted, the Northern Soul scene is massive once again. Every week there is a choice of somewhere to go. Soul clubs have opened up all over the country. Some small, like the Bushey Soul Club near Watford, and some huge like the King's Hall in Stoke. Apart from going worldwide with the Soulies underground ways of recruiting followers, the music has even reached Joe Public now, due to recent television adverts like the soul food Kentucky Fried Chicken advert where they use such sounds as "Moonlight, Music And You" by Laura Greene, "Do I Love You? Indeed I Do" by Frank Wilson. Another advert that comes to mind is the Felix cat food advert, where they use the 'choon' "You've Been Away" by Rubin. Us Soulies had no idea what we had twenty-five years ago but we certainly do now.

One evening, I went to the Bushey Soul Club and on this particular night, I was on my own. I had a little dance, looked in a few record boxes, as you do, then I met a really nice girl called Kay Seabrook, who has become one of my best friends. We spoke about the music and the dancing. I tried to explain to her that because the music was a lot slower now it was a bit more difficult to dance to. After watching Kay dance, I started to adjust my own style of dancing to suit the sounds I was hearing. Perhaps I did leave the Northern Soul scene a bit early and missed out on how the music was evolving into what we are hearing today. When I hear a DJ announce, 'Here we go with an old Casino classic,' I would turn round to Yogi and say, "I never heard this at Wigan Casino."

Yogi would say, "Well after we left, there was another four years' worth before the Casino closed."

My sister Jackie, me, and my brother Geoff.

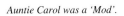

Auntie Carol was a 'Mod'.

Dad and I, hardly Ronnie Scott's material!

"Stacking system" record player.

Me wearing typical Torch clothes.

Debbie from Huddersfield, 1973.

The boys in the Casino: Reg, Yogi, John and half of Roland!

Quality time with the Shepherd family.

Me (with hair) in photo booth.

Junior Walker, live at the California Ballroom.

Buckie on his way to Wigan.

Roland and me in Wigan Casino.

It's only a copy of 'If You Ever Walk Out of My Life' by Dena Barnes.

Bev, Shirley, Sue, Karen and Curly in the Bali Hi.

Ange, Barbs and Jane, southern Soulies at their best.

The woman behind the little man on the dancefloor – my wife Debbie.

Shirley Holland wearing my designer ski jumper.

Skiing in the snow.

Early Caister.

21st birthday cake as requested. Thanks Mum!

Me and the girls in the Bali Hi.

*Scooter as
used on
CD cover.*

*'Sitting On The Dock Of The Bay' on a blue Stax.
Thanks again mum!*

Four hundred quid well spent!

Soul boys.

*Sounds of Soul DJ team.
Chris finally gets his Soul Club.*

With Caister's number one DJ
Peter Collins.

Lovely job Reg, thanks very much.

Ronnie O'Brien, Caisters' best looking DJ.

Reg on
the decks.

Gary, Shazza and Susie at Caister.

Blue Skies Soul Club

Kicking off the New Year
With a Special Night
Martin (Rbman) Ainscough's Birthday
13th January, 2006

Extra Special DJ Line Up

Arthur Fenn
Little Reg from Sounds of Soul
Mac from Soul in the City
John Stubbs, Geoff Green

Northern Soul, old and new, Motown 60s
classics and
R&B Mod Monsters

£5 otd

The Cranbourne Rooms
The Red Lion Hotel
Great North Road
Hatfield
AL9 5EU
7.30 til 12.30

Information phone line:
078 5164 0863

A DimWit Promotion

Charlie and the Angels at Caister.

Debbie from Huddersfield now.

Café Latté completed by Christmas.

Toby, me and Martin at Southgate 2006.

Last photo with mother.

Janie from Worcester is still with us.

Chilling out with our Emma at Caister.

I have no regrets about leaving when I did, as since then I've met so many different types of Soul fans and I now have a record collection that goes right across the board. Nowadays, I feel right at home in a Jazz bar, at a rave, Jazz funk club or a northern all-nighter. I'm comfortable in all these different types of venues, especially as I still recognise people from my past. It's as if everyone has been called back to his or her different types of soul clubs at the same time.

The soul fans of my age group have done the marriage bit and their kids are out clubbing themselves, or at least old enough to be left with Mum and Dad or baby sitters. It appears that we are all coming out to play again.

In the Northern Soul scene, the Soulies who are ten years younger than me have a wealth of information on the sounds that I have missed out on during the time I was away from the scene. I have been buying mid tempo tunes recently, which I like, and I feel that I am filling the gaps in my record boxes. The records are a lot dearer nowadays but that's what collecting things is all about. Like I said in one of the previous chapters, we had about two thousand records between us, but felt we needed some more, because when you're playing your music to the paying public, you try and cater for most of the Soulies, whatever age they are.

Our soul clubs at Nash Mills were brilliant while they lasted, but within three years things went pear-shaped. I'm afraid I'm a guy who strives for perfection and asked the punters if they had any ideas to make the soul club better, which didn't go down too well with Dave and we fell out. When this happened the numbers went down and Bennetts End Soul Club finally fizzled out. This didn't worry me that much, as I had plenty of different soul clubs to go to, especially when Kay told me she was going to help her mate Neil Oppegard run a new soul club called The North Herts 6Ts Mafia at the Plinston Hall, Letchworth.

At the Plinston Hall, they cater for all needs of specialised music: Mod, Jazz Crossover, Modern and of course Northern Soul. At present this club, along with the Ritz in Desborough, have become my favourites, mainly because instead of leaving the clubs as I did all those years ago, you just move rooms at the same venue to change the style of music.

On one particular night when Yogi and I had arranged to go to the Ritz at Desborough, I got a phone call from one of the Soulies who used to attend the Bennetts End do's. Her name was Michelle Bennett and she asked if she and her friend Chris Stanley could come with us.

I said, "No problem Miche. Be round my house at 8 o'clock sharp and I'm sure Yogi won't mind taking you both with us."

I had not met Chris before, but within the hour of travelling to Desborough it was quite apparent that Chris was led to the music by the scooter scene and the way he spoke, he was very knowledgeable about old scooters. It had seemed like Chris had reached the pinnacle of designing and rebuilding of scooters and now he was striving to reach a decent level of knowledge in the soul music scene. Chris was fascinated by our conversations about the old days and all the soul clubs we had visited.

When we arrived back in Hemel Hempstead, Chris said, "I'm definitely up for coming souling with you two again. It's been an experience. Where are you going next and can I come with you?"

"Of course you can," we replied, "but we don't go every week, we pick and choose the places we think we would like and sometimes it's as late as Saturday evening when Yogi phones, just like the old days."

"'Hey Reg it's me, we're out tonight if you're up to it, I'll be round about quarter to eight.'

"'Okay Mate, I'll be ready.'" (Nothing changes does it?) As long as you don't mind us phoning at short notice you can come anytime you want."

"Cheers lads," Chris replied, "and if you ever consider starting up another Soul Club let me know."

I thought to myself, 'Once bitten twice shy—I don't think that will happen.'

It only seemed like a couple of months later when Yogi and I were on our way to the 6Ts Mafia first anniversary at Plinston and as we were driving, I looked at Yogi and he looked at me and we both started laughing. Who would have thought we would be doing this all these years later and bumping into people we hadn't seen for ages? I often wondered if

Janie from Worcester was still with us, as no one had heard anything through the grapevine.

Whilst we were travelling I said to Yogi, "There's a dance competition tonight."

His reply was, "Reg, get real, we're in our late forties, we wouldn't stand a bleeding chance."

"But I know how to win Yogi."

"What do you mean, you know how to win?"

"It's easy. All you do is prance about on the dance floor and if you're the last one left you win."

"You are definitely away with the mixer Reg."

"We'll see," I said.

As usual it was a great night at the Plinston. When the dance competition started there were about eighty dancers on the floor. After the first record they picked out thirty and guess what Yogi and I were still there. I gave Yogi the thumbs up and he gave me that look of 'it won't be long before were gone mate'. Last twenty—both still there, last ten—both still there.

I said to Yogi, "That's it mate, what did I tell you, we can both retire gracefully now."

At the end of the last sound, they announced the winners in reverse order.

"Third is Little Reg from Hemel, runner up is Trickster from London and first is Carol Smith from Spalding."

Well, I walked back from the stage with my 15 quid and said, "I told you I knew how to win mate." Then we laughed our bleeding heads off.

Our new mate Chris Stanley strode over and said, "What are you two laughing about."

We replied, "Oh it's nothing mate."

Then he said, "Have you thought about starting up that soul club yet?"

I replied, "Don't worry Chris, you'll be the first to know if we do."

Yogi and I were souling at least twice a month and loving every minute of it. Both our wives Debbie and Lorraine reckoned we were trying to relive our youth and going through a mid-life crisis. So! Why Not! Thank God they don't know what the sounds cost nowadays.

"So how much was that copy of 'Too Late' by Mandrill then?"

"Oh just a couple of quid dear..."

How many of you record collectors have said the same to your respective partners? All of us at some time or another I think. We'll stick to the same story though, eh?

At this time I was also doing quite well in the scooter scene, I joined some of the SAS scooter club on the great London 'ride out'. The idea was to meet at Carnaby Street and from there we would scoot through London to Stanmore Hospital and deliver Easter eggs to the sick children. However, unknown to us, Claude Scooters, a famous scooter shop down on the Edgware Road, were making a documentary called 'Scooters' for the Sky channel *Men & Motors*. Whilst we were waiting for everyone to meet, out of hundreds of scooters Claudia, Claude's daughter asked who owned the small Vespa.

"I would like it in the film, can you wheel it out the front with your mate Gary's."

I was amazed—mine wasn't a patch on some of the others but it was mine she wanted and that's what she got. But it wasn't only the scooter she wanted in the film it was me as well.

A few months later, I got a phone call from Gary saying, "We're on the telly Reg, being interviewed in Carnaby Street." We were only on TV for a couple of minutes, but I felt a great sense of achievement—me, in the scooter world! But being a film star hasn't changed my life......

Due to being on the telly, I get a call from a guy making a MacDonald's' advert. He was asking if he could borrow my scooter. It all seemed quite 'legit', so I lent it for one day's work and when he returned it he gave me £100. I never saw the advert but I was able to buy some more records. Can't be bad, eh?

After this, the icing on the cake was when a company called Addiction were to launch a CD called *Suited and Booted* for the V2 record company. This time I got to go with my scooter to a Battersea film studio, one day for the still photos then another for the video. The CD was on sale to the public just before Fathers' Day and within the first two weeks, it was the best seller of the month. All I can say is at least something came good from my money troubles and I'm happy to say I still have my scooter and I have met a lot of people through owning it.

RECORDS BOUGHT AROUND THIS TIME

Independant Woman	Jan Jones
I'm The One To Do It	Laverne Baker
A Case Of Too Much Lovemaking	Gloria Scott
Pushing Love	Al Green
Something New To Do	Bobby Sheen
Lonely Lover	Marvin Gaye
Back By Popular Demand	Jean Schene Linier
You're My Lucky Number	Ronnie McNeir
Trippin' On Your Love	A Way Of Life
Don't Send Nobody Else	Ace Spectrum
Pressure	Drizabone
I Wish I Didn't Miss You	Angie Stone
I Can't Speak	Jimmy Bo Horn
Stolen Hours	Patrice Holloway
Take Me Girl I'm Ready	Eddie Mercury
Stormy	Diana Ross And The Supremes
I'm So Happy	Prince Phillip Mitchell
What's Wrong With Me Baby?	The Invitations
Save Your Love For A Rainy Day	The Van Dykes
Wade In Water	Marlena Shaw

Chapter 22

Another Birthday Party

In 2002, I started to plan my fiftieth birthday party. I drew up a list of people who I would like to attend and when my wife Debbie counted up the names there were over five hundred. The ideal place to hold an event of this size was the Hemel Hempstead Pavilion—it would have been perfect if they hadn't pulled the place down the year before. My next thought was the St. Albans Civic Centre. I gave them a ring as the venue could cater for a thousand but they didn't hire the place for private functions. My next thought was the Luton Rugby Club but on the same night I wanted to hire the place, the Talk of the South soul club had already hired it.

Feeling a bit despondent, I went round to see my Mum. Whilst having a cup of tea, my mum looked over and said, "What's up, Son?"

I said, "I'm trying to hire a hall for my fiftieth birthday Mum, but with all my new friends, added up with the people that came to my other parties, it's well over five hundred and I can't find a local hall big enough."

"Oh, that sounds brilliant," Mum said, "I hope I'm still here to see it, that will give me something to look forward to."

You see 'me mum' was given three months to live fifteen years ago due to having cancer. So my brother, sister, Dad and me would always give her something to live for. Through my brother upgrading her caravan, my sister taking her on a cruise ship, she always had something to look forward too and our methods appeared to be working, even the doctors were baffled as to how Mum was still with us.

After discussing the party situation with Mum and seeing how ill she was, I decided to hire the same hall where I held my twenty-first, which was only over the road from where she lived. The down side to this decision was that the Bennetts End Community Centre only held two hundred people max. I had to doctor my list, but at least, God willing, Mum would still be there.

During 2002, Yogi and I were souling nearly every other week. The clubs we were mostly going to were in the Northampton area or the Eastern region, Wellingborough, Desborough, Cambridge, St. Ives and Kettering. Every time we went out, we came back with records, loads of them. Also, on one occasion we saw Eddie Holman perform; although he was singing to backing tracks, and couldn't quite reach the high notes, his show was still good enough for me. We picked up quite a few sounds that were missing from our record boxes along with some selective new ones.

Before I knew it, the year had flown past. Mum was still with us and my birthday was just around the corner. I told Mum I didn't want a cake this time because I didn't want to stop the music to cut it, but really it was because she was too ill to make it. The party was a huge success, and the highlight of the evening was dancing with my Mum. All of my girlfriends who attended my party had a lump in their throats as the record we danced to was 'How Am I Supposed To Live Without You' by Michael Bolton. Although Mum was so ill, she managed to live a couple of years longer but this was to be my last dance with her.

A couple of days after the party, my mate Glen Colgate came round to my workshop and said, "All right Reg. Best party I've ever been to. The music! You pay a lot of money for that music don't you?"

"You could say that Glen," I replied.

"I said to my wife Jan, there wasn't a bad record all night. Brilliant. Oh by the way, I want to get you some of the cutters you use in your router machine for your birthday."

"You don't have to do that Glen, your presence was good enough."

"No I want to, show me the ones you need."

Whilst I was showing Glen the cutters he said, "That music was brilliant on Saturday Reg. What's your favourite at the moment?"

"You don't want to go there, Glen. My favourite at the moment is 'What Does It Take To Win Your Love' by The Electrifying Cashmeres. Manship records have got a copy, but it's £175."

"Fuckin' hell! What idiot will pay that kind of money?"

"Exactly," I said. "For that kind of money I can take my wife and kids to Southend for the day, stop at Lakeside on the way home and treat them all, so you can't comprehend it can you?"

"No, I see what you mean Reg. Anyway I'm off now I'll leave them cutters by your back door if you're not in."

"Don't worry Glen. As I said, your presence was good enough. Mind how you go, I'll see you soon."

Two days later when I got home from work I opened my back door and on the handle was a plastic shopping bag. I thought, "Old Glen has only gone and got them cutters," but it wasn't cutters inside the bag, it was a mint copy of 'What Does It Take To Win Your Love?' by The Electrifying Cashmeres.

I phoned Glen and said, "That was a lot of money Glen."

"Listen here, Shorts, I came into this world with fuck all, and I will go out with fuck all. Happy Birthday Son."

What could I say? Other than "Thanks very much!"

Yogi and Lorraine took me to see the play *Once Upon a Time in Wigan*. We did it in style, as they also bought us all a meal in a restaurant opposite the theatre before the performance. Another friend, Steve Cannon, took me to the Caister Soul Weekender; birthday presents of the highest quality. The different types of soul music could not be closer now, they even dedicated at least six hours to the Northern Soul scene (it's never been heard of before). During the Northern Soul afternoon I finally met my match, I was approached by two girls who were deeply into Soul music as much as I was, their names were Susanne and Sharon. The reason they came over to me was because I was dancing to a Northern Soul tune called 'Too Much Love Making' by Gloria Scott—a brilliant record which I have managed to get hold of recently. They wanted to know about the Northern Soul scene as they too had just seen the play, *Once Upon a Time in Wigan*. Meeting these girls was a massive bonus;

what they didn't know about Jazz Funk and Modern Soul wasn't worth knowing. Susanne asked if I had any records with me.

"Of course I have, I brought my record player as well. It's back in my chalet."

"You're not in one of those chalets? How the fuck did you manage that?"

"I don't know," I replied. "This weekend was a birthday present off me mate Steve"

Without hesitation Susanne said, "Sharon, get your jacket we're going round to Reggie's. He's only got his record player here and he's in one of those posh chalets."

So there I was walking back to my chalet with two stunning birds thinking I've had some birthday presents in my time, but this beats the lot! My mates were gobsmacked back in the main ballroom, thinking 'what's he got that we haven't'. I guess it was my records—it couldn't have been my looks—I'm 3-foot high and bald!

Whilst we were walking, Suzi whispered, "You haven't got a copy of 'I Wanna Give You Tomorrow' have you? It's Shaz's favourite?"

"Yes," I said, "It's in my record box, it's by Benny Troy, on a Delight label."

"Brilliant. What a sound! Don't tell her; just put it on," Suzi said.

Then we both turned round at the same time looking for Sharon and spontaneously started laughing. Sharon was about a hundred yards behind us waddling down the road, swearing like a trooper.

"Look at the state of her, Reg."

"How does she manage in those bloody great high heels?" I asked.

"Hurry up," Suzi shouted.

In the distance Sharon shouts, "It's me bloody shoes, ain't it."

Suzi said, "They're no good for walking but you wanna see her dance in them, she's a brilliant dancer."

I instantly knew at this moment that these girls were going to be mates for the rest of my life. You know when you meet someone who is exactly your cup of tea, with the same interests as you and a sense of humour to die for, these girls had it all. After they had a good look around our posh chalet, all three of us grabbed a beer each, I dragged the kitchen table to the nearby plug socket and placed my small record player and record box on the table.

"I don't believe it, where did you get that brilliant record player?"

"I bought it at a car boot sale, it was £8," I said.

"No you're having a laugh, £8, it's just cost me that for a couple of drinks, if you ever see another one will you get it for me?" Sharon asked. "Do you take it everywhere?"

"Of course I do, it runs on batteries as well, I even take it on camping holidays. Sit over there if your feet are hurting and I'll play you some of my sounds."

As Sharon and Suzi were new to the Northern Soul sounds, I played them some soulful classics such as: "Am I Cold, Am I Hot" by Bill Harris; "Sad Girl" by Carol Anderson; "Name It You Got It" by Mickey Moonshine; "Breakaway" by Steve Karmen; and "Let Her Go" by Otis. Smith.

Then I put on I 'Wanna Give You Tomorrow' by Benny Troy. As soon as it kicked in, Sharon jumped out of her seat and started prancing around. I had no idea how she danced as well as she did in those bloody great big high heels.

Then Sharon puts her hands in the shape of a letter T and shouts "Tune, what a tune!!"

I looked down at her fancy footwork and said, "Sharon, take it easy; your feet are bleeding, why don't you wear some flat comfortable shoes or a ballet shoe."

"No can't do that Reg I'm too small, I've gotta look my best when I'm out dancing however much pain I go through."

I must say both girls were absolutely stunning and in conversation it appeared that they certainly knew their music. We played a few more sounds: "She'll Come Running Back" by Mel Britt; "I Wish" by Angie Stone; and "It Will Never Be Over For Me" by Timmi Yuro.

After about an hour, we all went back to the main ballroom, where Suzi and Sharon introduced me to the rest of their mates, another three girls and two fellas. There was Nettie (Annette), Julie, Janet, Steve and Paul. I thought to myself, 'I've been here before, southern Soulies at their best. Is history repeating itself?' The difference this time was that the music was a lot closer, there seems to be an acceptance on both sides of the soul scene these days as I've said before, even at Caister. Instead of changing venues, I just change rooms. Everywhere across the country where soul music is being played, the proprietors are catering for all tastes.

Later in the evening, Sharon introduced me to one of Caister's top DJs called Peter Collins. Meeting Pete was like receiving another birthday pressie. What a smashing bloke he is, we got on like a house on fire, two peas in a pod. Within half an hour, Pete and his mates asked if I would like to go with them to the Togetherness weekender near Blackpool. I was gobsmacked. These guys were the tops where collecting soul music was concerned and I was blown away just to be considered to join their company at the Togetherness weekender.

I said to Pete, "I'll have to let you know nearer the time," which was fine with him.

On the Sunday, just before leaving to return back to Hemel, Steve, Susanne's brother, asked if I ever went to a soul club at the Haven hotel in St. Albans about twenty years ago.

"Of course I did," I replied "Why?"

Steve said, "I'm promoting a Haven reunion in a couple of weeks time and wondered if you would like to go."

"Definitely," I replied, "I'll fetch one of my girlfriends."

"How many have you got then, Reg?"

"Hundreds, Matey. I think I'll fetch my friend Sara. She's got a skinhead haircut, is covered in the most amazing tattoos and is absolutely bonkers on Jazz Funk music."

Steve's reply was, "Yeah alright mate, I'll believe it when I see her."

"Just put two tickets aside for us Steve I'll definitely be there, I'll give you a ring when I get back to Hemel so I know you all got home alright."

Travelling back home, all I kept thinking about was the brilliant time I'd had and the fantastic new friends I had just met.

As soon as I got back to Hemel, I phoned my mate Sara and asked, "How do you fancy a date with a three foot high, little, round, bald bloke?"

Sara's reply was, "What you got in mind then Reg?"

"I wondered if you would like to go to an evening of Jazz, Funk and Soul in St. Albans, Sara,"

"I'm definitely up for that Reg, if you take me to that do I'll wear my best skirt."

"Wow," I thought. "I've never seen Sara in a frock before, all she ever wears is jeans and T-shirts."

"When is it?" Sara asks.

"It's in two weeks' time."

"Oh, I'm working in the 'Odds' until six-thirty, I'll shower and change in the pub and you can meet me there Reg."

"No probs, if you're not ready I'll wait in the bar. Happy days then Sar?"

"No, I still haven't forgiven you for not taking me to Caister yet."

"Oh leave it out Sar! I'll take you next time. You know I was a guest, I was taken by my mates, it was a birthday present."

"I know Reg, just make sure you take me next time, ok?"

"I will."

Two weeks later, I strolled into the Oddfellows Arms and some of my mates were sitting at the bar. Trevor looks up and says, "Where are you off to, all dolled up?"

"Nowhere special mate, I've got a red hot date."

"What does your wife Debbie say about that then?"

"Oh, she just told me to behave myself."

"I don't know Reg, you've got it made, Son."

"Well the difference between me and you Trev, is I do behave myself. You haven't seen Sara have you Trev?"

"Yeah she's just finished her shift she's got a date as well, I don't know who she's seeing but he must be special, she reckons she's gonna wear her skirt."

"Really? You're having a laugh Trev. I've only ever seen her in jeans."

"Yeah same as that Reg, I've only ever seen her in jeans as well."

A couple of minutes later, in walked Sara. Trevor and the other lads were gobsmacked. She looked stunning. She was wearing a low cut T-shirt with a dainty looking skirt which she had made herself. With her closely cropped hair and her tattoos of fairies dancing from her shoulders to her waist, Sara walked over to me and whispered in my ear, "I brush up all right, don't I?"

I replied, "You can say that again sister." I grab her hand and said to the lads, "I'll see yer later," and walked out of the pub.

When we arrived at the Quality Hotel where the Haven reunion was being held, Sharon, Susanne and Janet were on the door. As we walked down a small corridor Susanne shouts, "He's here, Reg is here." I must say these girls really know how to make their friends feel really special. Then I introduced Sara to the girls, we paid for our tickets then entered the dance area. Steve and Pete Collins were working the decks. We got some drinks and found a table near the disco area.

Once we started dancing, we never left the floor all night—the music was outstanding.

They played such sounds as: "Dominoes" Donald Byrd; "Daylight" Bobby Womack; "Take It To The Top" Kool And The Gang; "Every Day" Sunburst Band; "Love To The Music" The Temptations; "Where Will You Go When The Party Is Over?" Archie Bell And The Drells; "The Love I Lost" Harold Melvin & The Bluenotes; "Here I Go Again" Archie Bell And The Drells.

The list was endless—every one a gem. The night was just like a mini Caister. When Sara and I left at the end we could hardly walk.

Sara said, "That was one of the best nights I've ever had, my legs are killing me, I loved it Reg. Thanks."

Then I said to Sara, "Do you think you could dance from twelve noon to four o'clock in the morning, for three days on the trot? If you think you can, it's only then you will qualify for Caister."

RECORDS BOUGHT AROUND THIS TIME

My Life	Chanel
Making My Daydream Real	We The People
Overdose Of Joy	Eugene Record
Travelling On	Chestnut Brothers
Let's Get It On (Remix)	Marvin Gaye
I'd Rather Leave On My Feet	Emanuel Laskey
My Good Friend James	The Pioneers
Come Get To This	Marvin Gaye
The Whole Darn World Is Going Crazy	John Gary Williams
What Does It Take?	Electrifying Cashmeres
Ordinary Joe	Terry Callier
My Proposal	Soul Inc
Pyramid	Soul Brothers Inc
Top Of The Stairs	Collins & Collins
This Love Affair	Gloria Gaynor
Don't Send Nobody Else	Ace Spectrum
Soul On Wax	Mr Day
Party Time Man	The Fugitives
Pressure	Drizabone
Crazy World	Kenny Thomas

Chapter 23

Chris Finally Gets His Soul Club

Between 2003 and 2004, I was souling at the highest level. There are so many do's going on nowadays I am spoilt for choice, especially as I go right across the board where soul music is concerned. If I'm going to a Northern Soul do, I'll always see if Yogi's up for it and we'll travel together. If anyone else wants to come with us, they're quite welcome; we can normally fit five in Yogi's car but most of the time it's just the two of us. This is mainly because sometimes we don't even know if we are going out until the Saturday afternoon, so it's pretty short notice really and most of our mates have already made other arrangements.

On the other hand, if I fancy going to a Jazz Funk evening, all I have to do is ring Sharon or Suzanne to see if they are going to the Vevo's Soul club. Suzanne normally hires a mini bus. The Hemel crew (Sara Jane, Leroy and me) arrange to meet at Sharon's flat where we have a quick glass of wine whilst waiting for Suzanne, Nettie and the others to arrive in the mini bus. Vevo's is a club situated right by St. Paul's Cathedral. When you enter, the cash desk is right by the front door, then you walk down a small flight of steps. On the left hand side is where you enter what we call the top bar. Opposite the entrance to the top bar is a spiral staircase to the dance floor and downstairs bar.

At Vevo's you meet most of the Caister Soulies and some of Caister's top DJs such as the infamous Pete Collins along with Ronnie O'Brian, Maggot, Shifty and Big Man Harvey. All these DJs have become great friends of mine through knowing Sharon, Suzanne and Nettie. I've always had great nights at Vevo's, because just like the Northern Soul scene, the people are brilliant and so is the music. The DJs, who are now my mates, seem to break new 'choons' at venues like Vevo's, Lacy Ladies or some of the other jazz funk clubs. Then if the new sounds are a huge success in the smaller clubs they will take them to Caister which, in my opinion, is the heart of the new Jazz Funk scene at the moment. Another thing I like about going to Vevo's is, if you want to cool off during the evening, you can have a nice leisurely stroll around St. Paul's Cathedral, which is all lit up during the night.

I still find I'm attending more Northern Soul do's than the Jazz Funk ones, but drifting between the two makes a pleasant change and I get to clock in with all my mates, which is the most important part of it all to me.

One night, Yogi and I arranged to meet Chris and his new girlfriend (also called Lorraine) at the Bisley Pavillion. This soul club is called the Nightshift Club. We all had a fantastic night there, as it happened to be our friend Kay Seabrook's birthday. As we entered this magnificent venue, looking at the stage on the left-hand side, Kay had saved about four tables for all her birthday guests. Whilst my friends Jenny, Chris and the rest of the Soulies were fluffing around her with cards and pressies, I caught her attention and just walked straight past her without saying a word. The look on her face said it all! I waited for the small frenzy to die down, then slowly walked back to where Kay was standing. I carefully placed my soul bag on the table, undid the zip and as I parted the bag with my hands a glow appeared. At the great expense of nearly catching all my fucking clothes on fire, I lifted out a small cake with the candles already alight and said, "Happy Birthday Sister."

Kay's words were, "You rotten sod, I thought you'd forgotten me."

I replied, "I wouldn't dream of forgetting your birthday after the look you just gave me."

Later during the evening Chris came over to where Yogi and I was standing and said, "Well I'm not waiting any longer, are you in or out? If you don't want to start up another Soul club, I'm going to run one on my own."

"What do you think Reg?" said Yogi.

"Providing that if we have any problems like last time, instead of it all falling apart, we all sit down, talk about it and sort it out."

Then Yogi says, "OK. Are we all free next Saturday and can you both raise about 500 quid each?"

Chris replied, "No problem. What about you Reg?"

"Yeah, I've got it in my tax book," and we all shook hands.

Yogi says to Chris, "It looks like you've got yourself a Soul Club, matey."

By the look on Chris's face, you would have thought he was a pools winner. I must admit I was quite excited about the whole prospect too.

The following week we all went to Chris's house about 9.30am and set off to buy the DJ equipment. First port of call was a DJ shop in St. Albans. On the way there, Yogi mentioned that during the previous week he had been doing a bit of homework on DJ shops in our area. "So we'll see what the bloke has to say in St. Albans then we'll nip over to Dunstable; that's the next nearest shop."

When the bloke added the price of the equipment that we quite liked, the total price was £2,200; and that figure was with our cash discount. It was a bit more than we had budgeted for, so we headed over to Dunstable. The price of the DJ equipment at Dunstable was within our budget around the £1,375 mark, so the deal was struck.

After loading the equipment into the car, the three of us called into a café for breakfast, all feeling quite pleased with our purchase. We then headed back to Chris's house. Once Chris and Yogi had set up the DJ equipment, I was allowed to play the first sound. Instead of a Northern Soul record, I placed my twelve inch copy of 'Happy People' by R. Kelly on the turntable. The record kicked in and the sound was perfect, just like when I bought my first stereo from Tottenham Court Road. You could hear sounds you wouldn't normally hear on a less expensive set-up and my choice of record was quite apt, as in this case there were three happy people. After we all had a turn spinning our sounds, we disconnected the speakers as Yogi volunteered to store them at his house.

Sitting in Yogi's living room, having a cup of tea, Chris asked, "What are we going to call the Soul Club?"

All three of us liked the record 'SOS' by Edwin Starr. We wrote the letters SOS on a piece of paper and tried to think of a name using these letters. We wracked our brains for about half an hour and couldn't come up with any ideas. Just as we were about to change the format, Yogi's youngest son Nick shouts out what about 'Sounds of Soul'. The three of us all looked at each other gobsmacked, then I said, "That's it! Brilliant Nicks, that's what we'll call our new Soul Club."

SOUNDS OF SOUL!

Chapter 24

Sharing Company with the Rolls-Royce of Soul Collectors

In the November of 2004, I got a phone call from my old mate Peter Collins asking if I was up for going to the Togetherness Weekender in Blackpool. After speaking with Debbie about the weekend and getting her approval, it was all systems go.

I phoned up the train station but the fare was too expensive, so I asked Sharon and Suzanne if there was enough room in their car, but the spare seat Suzanne had was taken up by Sharon's work colleague called Lisa. I thought, I don't really want to drive to Blackpool on my own but if I have to I will, as offers like this don't come up very often.

After a couple of days I got another phone call from Steve, Suzanne's brother saying that he was taking his van to Blackpool and would I like to travel up with him. Now I know Steve is nowhere near as good looking as Sharon and Suzanne, but beggars can't be choosers, so that's what I did. Steve left Southampton where he lives about 8 o'clock and arrived at my house in Hemel Hempstead about 11.30am. After a sandwich and a quick cup of tea we loaded up Steve's van with my weekend stuff. My Soul bag contained plenty of clothes, swimmers, wash bag etc, then in went a small record box which contained about fifty sounds, a couple or three 12inch singles and finally my small record player.

Steve said, "I can't believe you're taking that little record player with you."

I replied, "Oh it's dead handy to have on board Steve, especially if we are thinking of buying some records in Blackpool, 'cos we'll be able to play them straight away. Also, I want to wind up Pete Collins and the others by playing strictly vinyl in the caravan."

Once we got rolling, Steve started playing some top 'choons' on the CD player in his van and in no time at all we were transferring from the M1 to the M6 heading towards Lancashire. After about two-and-a-half hours we arrived at the holiday park where the Togetherness Weekender was being held. Our timing was impeccable; as we got out of Steve's van, a taxi pulled up behind us with Pete Collins and all the other lads, so the eight of us that were sharing the same caravan were all together in the queue waiting to get our weekend passes. Once we had our passes Steve and I headed back to get his van while the others looked for where the caravan was situated. Luckily enough it was not too far from the main dance hall, so everything was sweet.

Whilst the rest were sorting out where everyone was sleeping in the caravan, I disappeared for about fifteen minutes, then about fifty yards from the caravan I placed my copy of 'Crazy World' by Kenny Thomas on my portable record player. (This isn't an easy thing to do as the 12-inch singles overlap the sides of the actual player itself.) I lowered the stylus onto the piece of vinyl and as soon as the 'choon' kicked in, I carefully walked towards the caravan.

All of a sudden the lads jumped out of the caravan to see where the music was coming from; they all start laughing their heads off, then Pete Collins says, "I don't know Reg, what a crack-up you are. He's like one of them market traders—you hear him before you see him. Absolutely brilliant and what a 'choon' as well."

Once we all got settled down and had a cup of tea and something to eat, I started to realise the amount of knowledge that these lads had in the world of Soul music. Although their tastes were slightly different, every time someone played a 'choon' someone would say "What a sound! Where the fuck did you get a 'choon' like that?"

Then the owner of the particular 'choon' in jest would say, "Never you mind, it's gold dust."

The chap making the enquiry would then say, "You rotten bastard. I'll get a copy one day."

The banter was like this all weekend and it was always about the music but if I made a fuss about a certain sound I liked, the owner would say, "Don't worry Reggie I'll copy it for you." Or they would tell me exactly where to get a copy, providing I didn't tell the other lads where to get one. I think it was because these lads were tops where Soul music was concerned and just like the Northern Soul followers, they got tremendous pleasure of owning a 'choon' that no one else had. Even if it happened to be on a CD it didn't matter. Also because I was a Northern Soul fan, where this small competition was concerned, I didn't enter the equation. If I liked one of their records they did their very best to get it for me.

What was different about this weekend was that everyone was so relaxed. There was no worrying about trivial things like all having something to eat on time or a panic for the bath water, or what time we were going out; no one seemed to mind, they just came and went as they pleased. One of the reasons for this might have been that it was an all-nighter and they knew that sometime during the night they would all be having a drink and a dance together but whatever time that was going to be, didn't matter. Or, it might have been that the music the eight of us had between us was better than what was being played at the venue!

I came to the conclusion that I was sharing company with the Rolls-Royce of soul collectors. If these lads got an old tent in the middle of a field, a crate of beer and something to play their 'choons' on, they would be in paradise, happy as sand boys. Also if you weren't having something to eat, having a wash or getting ready to go out, you were either playing your set of records to everyone else or listening to what was being played. This truly was a weekend for the connoisseurs of Soul music and I felt privileged to be a part of it all.

I had heard so many brilliant 'choons' and I hadn't even stepped one foot outside of the caravan yet. We were still dawdling around at 9pm. Although most of us were ready to go out, we were quite content just sitting in and listening to the 'choons' chatting about the music. It was about 9.30 when a small frenzy occurred due to a phone call from Suzanne asking where we were. The three girls and another friend called Gary had arrived and were waiting in the Modern room. So those of us that were ready to go out, went to meet them straight away while the others got ready and followed on later. Whilst we were strolling towards the venue, I realised I was the only one carrying a bag. I said, "Don't you lads get changed during the evening."

Lovely Dave replied, "No we don't have to, our dancing isn't 100 miles an hour like yours Reg, we just bop on the spot, we hardly break into a sweat, whereas your lot come out of the discos wringing wet. I don't know how you dance like you do at your age. All that hand clapping, back dropping, spinning and shuffling across the floor."

I replied, "Sometimes I wonder myself Dave, we're obviously nowhere near as agile as we were thirty-odd years ago but you hear a certain 'choon' and it sends you instantly back in time. It makes you think that you are in your teens again and you just have to get on that dance floor. You still feel the music with the same passion and think you are dancing like you used to, but I bet we are nowhere near as good as we think we are!"

Once we arrived in the Modern room, I couldn't wait to see Sharon and Suzanne, I really love these two girls as I've said before; they are exactly my cup of tea. After spending an hour there, I had to go and pay the main room a visit. I asked if any of the crew wanted to come with me, but the music being played in the Modern room was exceptional and everyone was happy where they were.

As I went to pick up my bag it weighed a ton, then some of the lads started laughing they had only filled it up with empty beer bottles. I started laughing myself then I thought, 'Oh shit, I've got some of my rare records in the bag.' I quickly removed the bottles to examine my elusive pieces of vinyl and thank God they were all okay.

Susie said, "Go on then Reg I'll come with you, as long as I can flit between the two rooms that will be good." As Susie and I entered the main room, on the right hand side was the Gold Soul record stand, which was quite busy with people buying records. I recognised Kev Roberts and his wife. They had obviously changed a bit from the old days from when I knew Kev at Wigan. Then his looks were more of the hippy type with his hair touching his shoulders but not anymore; it's starting to disappear like most of us Wiganites. We are well into our fifties, I have no hair at all now but at least we still have the music running through our veins and the same passion we had all those years ago.

I looked at the dance floor. I was so disappointed; it was only one of those makeshift floors made up of sections! I thought, 'how can you hold an event of this size on a crappy dance floor like that?' Sooner or later someone is going to have a serious accident on one of these dance floors. Sometimes the sections would come apart leaving gaps and the sides of these floor sections have metal strips. You can't spin and slide like you normally do because when the sole of your shoe hits the metal trim, you come to an abrupt stop therefore you can't get lost in your music, because most of the night you are too busy worrying about falling on your arse.

I looked at Suzanne and said, "The floor is a bit crap but we won't let it spoil our weekend will we?"

Suzanne's reply was, "Is the floor that important Reg?"

"It would have been thirty years ago Suzanne. Thirty years ago it would have been a serious matter if we had waited all week to go souling and were presented with a floor like that. We would have been as miserable as sin, pissed-off big time and our mood wouldn't have changed for at least a week or until the next time we went souling. You see we lived for the dancing and the music but many of us didn't appreciate what was going on around us. We never took any photos or had time for many conversations, even our relationships were short-lived because most of our time was spent on the dance floor. But nowadays, if the floor is crap or the music isn't right, it does still affect me, but not as bad as it used to. I can now even have nights when I don't dance at all. I take in the bits that I missed in the past. The most important part to me now is the people. You will learn a lot tonight about the Northern Soul scene just by talking to the people."

"But I don't know any of them Reg."

"Oh, you will Suzanne. By the time you go back to that Modern room, you'll know at least twenty people minimum. Right what we'll do, we'll get a drink and then I'll take you to meet some of my mates."

Once we had got a drink the first person I introduced Suzanne to was Kenny Burrell the infamous DJ who paid £15,000 for that record 'Do I Love You, Indeed I Do' by Frank Wilson.

Suzanne said, "Shall we have a dance? I want to show you my new dance steps I've been practising."

"Okay sister, we'll dance by the left hand side of the stage where all my mates are."

As soon as Suzanne and I reached the place where we were going to dance, the DJ—who I didn't recognise—was playing 'Don't Let The Door Hit Your Back' by The Cashmeres. When the record finished Suzanne said, "Who's the brilliant dancer in the white trousers Reg?"

"That's our Emma, I'll take you over to meet her, the guy next to her is her boyfriend Tim Brown. He collects records in a very big way. Oh, I can also see Glen and the two girls from Bedford, Lorraine Allman and Chris Benson. I'll introduce you to them as well."

Just as we were walking over to where Emma was standing, the DJ played 'Ain't No Mountain High Enough' by Marvin Gaye and Tammi Terrell, so we had to dance. Five records later, Suzanne finally meets Emma, Tim and all the rest of my mates. Then I took Suzanne record hunting on Shaun Chapman's record stall.

Suzanne asked, "Is there any particular title you're looking for Reg?"

"Not really sister, I have a few record titles logged in my head but I don't think they will be on Shaun's record stall tonight. The ones I want are probably in his private collection at home."

Then I saw a sound that I've been after for a while, the instrumental to 'I'm Comin Home In The Morn'un' by Lou Pride. I particularly like the sound of the Hammond organ and it's slightly jazzy.

I removed the record out of the pack then Suzanne says, "It's been brilliant Reg just as you said. I've learnt a lot about the Northern Soul scene in just a couple of hours but I'm gonna have to go back to the Modern room now 'cos me boyfriend's gonna wonder where I've been."

"Okay, but before I walk you back, cop hold of this bundle of records for a second."

Whilst Suzanne was holding about fifty records, I placed the copy of 'Coming Home' by Southwind Symphony flat in the bottom of Shaun's record box and I stacked the ones that Suzanne was holding carefully on top.

Suzanne said, "You cheeky sod."

"Well it's the only way I can guarantee it will still be there when I come back!"

After seeing Suzanne back to the modern room, I returned to the main hall and purchased 'Coming Home' from Shaun. Then I went to the Gold Soul record stand. I spoke to a cracking looking girl called Becky who was in charge of the trade side of the company called Ibex. I told her I was running a Soul club with a couple of mates and I had a hundred pounds to spend. So between us we sorted out some of the latest reissues at a very good price, then I thought to myself, now I have some 'choons' for Chris to kick-start his record collection with.

I spent the rest of the night on my own until about 4am when I started to walk across the dance floor towards the Modern room to see if any of the lads were still up.

All of a sudden a voice said in a Yorkshire accent, "Hey you, are you Reggie from Hemel Hempstead?" as I turned around I thought, 'Oh my God; it's Debbie from Huddersfield'. A lot taller than me nowadays and still as good looking, I hadn't seen Debbie since the night I left Wigan Casino. I was gobsmacked for a few seconds then I said to her, "I loved you when we were kids."

Debbie pulled at her wedding ring jokingly and said, "Well why didn't you focking say owt then?"

We both sat and chatted for about an hour. We swapped phone numbers and agreed to keep in touch. It seemed that even after twenty-odd years the conversations carried on where we had left them.

Just after 5am, I made my way back to the Modern room where Pete Collins and Alan were still dancing. I placed my Soul bag under the table and said to the lads, "Don't fill my bag up with empties this time, it's full of vinyl."

Pete peeps in the bag and said, "Fucking hell he's not joking."

"Leave it under the table and we'll have a good sort out in the morning."

The three of us danced to every record played in the last hour, then when we were walking back to the caravan at about quarter past six, I thought that was one of the best times I had ever had, even though the floor was crap in the main room.

The only down side to this special night was that Yogi wasn't there with me to witness it.

Chapter 25

Sounds Of Soul

A few weeks after returning from that brilliant weekend in Blackpool, Chris and I started looking for an appropriate venue for the new soul club. I wish all the Soulies running other soul clubs that have started up recently approached the situation in the same way we did. The dance floor is the main priority, then it's the venue. Is it big enough? How many people does it hold? Does it have its own bar and staff or do we have to hire them in? What time do we have to stop playing the music? And finally, the car parking facilities.

Over the last thirty-odd years, everywhere that Yogi and I have been involved in holding Soul events; we've never had a bad dance floor. We had no problem when we used the Bennetts End Youth Club as we'd been dancing on that floor for the last forty-odd years. Although the youth clubs get refurbished now and then, the builders never seem to tamper with the floor surfaces. Then there was Nash Mills Hall; once again this venue had a superb real wood dance floor, good parking, the place was in the middle of nowhere and the only down side was you had to hire in a bar. We had to ask the Soulies to fetch their own drink, which turned out to be quite popular, so all in all it was not a bad venue at all. The only reason we didn't use Nash Mills Hall this time is because this was the place we were using when Bennetts End Soul Club started going downhill. So the three of us Yogi, Chris and I agreed it might be better to start Sounds of Soul at a fresh new place, if we could find a dance floor that would fulfil our needs.

I thought about Bennetts End Community Centre where I held most of my birthday parties. This venue has a brilliant dance floor but the parking is rubbish and it is situated close to some old people's flats, so there may have been a noise problem when the Soulies were leaving late at night.

The next venue we looked at was another village hall, which had only been built within the last five years called the Bedmond Village Hall. All three of us went to see the place. On arrival, the first thing we noticed was the car park, which was quite sufficient for the size of the venue. The place looked a bit small from the outside but on entering the building, the dance floor sold it to us.

I said to Chris and Yogi. "What do you think about the size?"

Yogi's reply was, "It will hold about 100 to 130 max. But if we only get thirty through the door we'll still have a good time. We'll start small, then if we have a couple of sell-outs we'll think about moving. You can be in charge of ticket sales Reg, as you know the world. Just keep Chris and I informed on how it's going."

So, we all agreed we'd use Bedmond Village Hall for a couple of do's and see how it went. Within a couple of days Yogi had designed the tickets. I personally thought they were brilliant, they were similar to airline tickets, long and skinny. Printed on the ticket was the information about the do and our logo 'SOUNDS OF SOUL'.

Within five minutes of Yogi dropping them off, my friend Michelle Bennett called round to buy the first two. She said, "Reg I always want number one and two, even if one day I can't go, I always want one and two."

Then Yogi phoned me up and said, "I've got another little job for you, we need a sign for the front of the disco. See what you can do."

On the Thursday night, two days before the grand opening of Sounds Of Soul, the three of us arranged to meet at Chris's house. Whilst Yogi and Chris set up the equipment for a practise, I tallied up the ticket sales.

"Ninety-four tickets sold, plus some promises on the door," I shouted.

"Bloody hell," Chris yelled, "at this rate we'll pay for the disco equipment in no time at all. Well done. What about the sign, did you manage to do it?"

"Yes," I replied, "it's in my car—I'll go and get it."

Whilst the boys were setting up the speakers I quietly placed the sign in front of Chris's settee then said, "Well, what do you think lads?"

They both looked up. Spontaneously Chris says, "That's great Reg," but it was Yogi's approval I was waiting for and after a long eight seconds Yogi looks at me and says, "Brilliant Reg, it's perfect." I thought to myself, 'Thank God that he likes it'.

The first Sounds Of Soul event was a huge success, another thirty tickets sold on the door—total number one hundred and twenty four—the whole affair was better than we could ever have imagined. Everyone had a brilliant time and was asking when the next do was. Also, I was well happy with the 'choons' I'd chosen for my one hour playing time.

On the Friday before the event I phoned up my mate Jenny Knight, as she works next door to a small record shop. I asked her if she could get me a copy of 'Ain't No Mountain High Enough' by Marvin Gaye and Tammi Terrell.

Jenny's reply was, "That sound isn't very rare Reg."

"I know it isn't, but I'm thinking of always finishing my set with an 'old Soul classic' and on this occasion I'd like it to be 'Ain't No Mountain High Enough'."

"Brilliant," she replied. "I'll see what I can do."

And, true to her word, ten minutes before I was about to take over from Chris, Jenny passes me the record.

"What do I owe you Jenny?" I asked.

"Call it a pressie, providing every time you play it, you play it for me."

So when I came to play my last sound of the evening, my words were, "Thanks for dancing. Thanks for singing. Thanks for listening. I'd like to finish with an 'old soul classic' and it's especially for my lovely mate, Jenny."

After the record had finished, I had a huge round of applause and felt quite pleased with my efforts. Once Yogi had started playing his set, I got straight back on the floor and said to Jenny, "Did you like your lovely record Jenny?"

She said, "You're a right creep you are Reg."

We just can't get it right can we lads? Even when we do exactly what the female of the species asks.

There was something else that happened on our first night of Sounds Of Soul, which was very special and will stay with me for the rest of my life. My friend Malcolm Apted phoned me up prior to the event and told me some very bad news about his wife Tracy; she didn't have long to live.

He said, "She has good days and bad days Reg,"

I replied, "Okay mate, is there anything I can do?"

"Well," said Malcolm, "Tracy has always wanted to see Northern Soul dancing, what do you think?"

I said, "If Tracy is having a good day fetch her along, it might make her feel a bit better. I'll look forward to seeing you and if you're not there I'll know Tracy's not feeling very well."

Whilst I was dancing to Yogi's brilliant set, I looked across the floor and saw Tracy smiling, sitting at a table.

I walked over to her and she said, "I bloody love it Reg, the dancing is amazing."

I asked Tracy, "How are you?"

"I'm not bad today Reg,"

"Well," I said, "you are not just going to watch then, you are going to dance with them as well. Give me your arm, I'll help you up."

I showed Tracy a few small steps and we danced to 'What' by Judy Street.

Our dancing lasted about forty seconds then Tracy whispered, "I'm gonna have to stop now, do you think they'll have dancing like this in heaven, Reg?"

"Of course they will sister, and when I get there, we'll finish our dance off."

Tracy grinned and said, "That will be lovely mate."

Sadly, a few weeks later Tracy passed away and when Malcolm told me, he said, "Tracy really loved the Northern Soul night Reg. She thought it was brilliant."

So that we could contact people about our next do, Yogi printed up some address and email sheets. Just before our next do, I was working my way through the names when I came across the one Tracy had filled in with her address and email. (I've kept that piece of paper ever since).

The next do that we held at Bedmond Village Hall was on a par with the first, except this time we were graced with the presence of some of the connoisseurs of the scene, such as Tim Brown, Emma Hagans, Neil Obergarrd and Karen Bedford. I've never seen Tim Brown dance, but the other three are exceptional dancers and appeared to be having a great time. Also as Tim Brown owns his own record company and writes for the Northern Soul magazine *Manifesto* I thought it would be good to get his opinion on our little Soul club.

During the time I was selling the tickets prior to the event my mates asked, "Will we be having another 'old soul classic'?"

"Of course we will," I told them, "I'll have to dig one out."

Whilst Yogi, Chris and I were sorting out our play list and checking out the equipment Chris asks, "What's your 'old soul classic' then Reg?"

I replied, "'Everything Is Tuesday' by Chairman Of The Board. I'm thinking of playing it for my friend Tracy who died."

"Do you think that would be a wise thing to do when everyone is enjoying themselves?"

"We'll see mate, I'll assess the situation at the time."

On the night of the do, when I get to my last sound, I looked up to heaven and said, "I'd like to dedicate my 'old Soul classic' to my friend Tracy who danced at our last do but sadly is no longer with us. So if you're looking down on me sister, this one's for you."

As soon as the record kicked in and General Johnson sings *'my heart was a lonely house where strangers wandered in and out'* the floor went wild. The Soulies danced like they'd never danced before. I looked down at my mate Jenny Knight dancing, she looked up at me with a tear trickling down the side of her cheek and gave me the thumbs up.

I smiled and thought, 'There's not many people that can dig that deep into their Soul whilst dancing and thinking about someone she never knew, but if anyone could, it would be our Jenny every time.' You see it's not just about the music. It's about the way we all feel about each other. Being a Soul music fan is very special, we listen to so many lyrics about the way people struggle through life, we learn how to feel other people's pain and I think that is why we're all so close.

Shortly after the do, I phoned up my mate Kay Seabrook to get her thoughts on how it went, as Kay helps run the Plinston Soul Club.

"Brilliant Reg; loved the 'old Soul classic'. I bet your friend was pleased with that 'choon' as well. The floor was busy too; everything was good apart from that bloody bar. No vodka and not much choice of drink either. And the prices! Expensive or what?! But I suppose that's what you get when you have to hire the bar in. Still, you can't have it all Reg, you've got three out of four right, brilliant dance floor, brilliant 'choons', lovely people but a shit bar. Never mind mate—apart from the bar I loved it."

Chapter 26

Sounds Of Soul: The New Venue

A week after the Sounds Of Soul do held at the Bedmond Village Hall, Chris and Yogi and I had a small meeting regarding comments made by our mates, either on the World Wide Web via *Soul Source* or via the phone. On the *Soul Source* website (www.soul-source.co.uk), there is a page called Events Talk where you can kick off your next Soul night by letting the Soulies know how the tickets are going; where the next do is; how to get there; starting and finishing times and so on. This part of the Sounds Of Soul club is Chris's department.

Chris (Dr. Pickles) starts the page off by announcing the Sounds Of Soul club are promoting another Soul night and gives all the details. Within minutes, Soulies wishing to come along join the web page. The first reply is normally one of our mates, a DJ called Mr Mischief. He will say in jest, "Hi lads, I see you're having another crappy Soul night, put me down for a couple of tickets, I like a good laugh."

A few minutes later, another one of our mates, normally Kay (Boots) will enter the page with something like, "Hi lads, it's me Boots, if your do is gonna be as crappy as Mischief says I would like a couple of tickets too."

Within a couple of days, the web page starts getting longer and longer with loads of other Soulies wishing to attend and most saying 'can I come to the crappy Soul do as well please?' A couple of days prior to the event the mood of conversation changes to Soulies, asking, "How are you getting there?"; "Is there any room in your car?"; "Is anyone driving past Potters Bar?"; "I need a lift as well"; "Are there any tickets left?"; "Can you reserve them on the door?" And so on. At this point, the *Soul Source* page hits its full frenzy, then we have the Soul night.

The day after the event, you switch on your computer, go into the same web page and see what the Soulies thought about how the do went. I must say that most who attend the Sounds Of Soul club really give positive feedback, which is very encouraging especially when coming from the connoisseurs of the Soul Scene. People such as Winston (Winnie) who has been Souling for quite a long time and through experience knows exactly what he's looking for in a Soul night out. Then, of course, the views of the two comedians will pop up—Mischief and Boots.

"Hi Boots, what did you think of the crappy Soul night out then?"

"Hi Mischief, it was crappy wasn't it, I've already got my tickets for the next one though."

"How did you manage that Boots? I thought I was the Sounds Of Soul number one fan. You wait till I see them I'm gonna have a go, getting your tickets before me! That's it. I've got the hump."

As I was saying, a week after our last Sounds Of Soul do, I met up with Yogi and Chris. I said to Yogi, "What's occurring then?"

"Well," Yogi replied, "we're gonna try and get the four out of four right Reg. It wasn't only Kay saying 'brilliant dance floor, brilliant 'choons', lovely people but shit bar'. It seems everyone loved the Soul do, but was disappointed with the bar."

I replied, "But whatever bar we hire in we've got no control over it have we?"

Then Yogi said, "I know it's a bit previous to our plans, but we need a venue with its own bar and staff. We are getting a hundred and thirty through the door at Bedmond. If we can get a place that can hold 200 plus, with its own bar and staff we will be laughing. What's the best floor you've danced on locally?"

"Well," I replied, "it's got to be Hemel Town Football Club. It's owned by David Boggins but it's a three hundred pound venue."

Yogi, being good at maths, immediately said, "Sixty tickets at a fiver each will cover the price of the hall, anything over the top will go towards the cost of the equipment. We all said at the start that all three of us were prepared to pay fifty quid each for a Soul night out at our own club if the numbers were low, so let's go for it. At least we could make the dance floor smaller by putting the tables closer if we had to. Are any of us in a hurry tonight?"

"Not really," Chris and I replied. "Well let's go and have a look at the place then."

On arrival at Hemel Town F.C. we first noticed that the car park was massive. It could hold about six coaches along with loads of cars as well. When we entered the room, it had a superb dance floor made of real wood (maple) and stretched across the full width of the venue—a wall-to-wall dance floor—it couldn't have been better. Then there was the bar area. Between the bar and the dance floor was a counter set up, which encourages anyone waiting for a drink to form an orderly queue. Also, the drinks were at working men's club prices, which would obviously please the Soulies. Next was the huge stage area, which was perfect; nice and big so when you set up the equipment, there was plenty of room for a couple of record tables. Another thing we liked about the place was it was very similar to a really successful Soul club called the Right Track in Peterborough, which all three of us attended on a regular basis.

Yogi asked the man behind the bar, "What time do you have to be out of here if you hire the hall mate?"

"Last record at midnight."

"Well if that's the only down side lads, we'll start at seven, especially if people are coming from a long way away."

Then I asked Yogi and Chris if they would like a drink and we sat down for a chat.

Yogi said, "It's perfect Reg,"

"I can't believe it's so much like Peterborough," said Chris.

Then I replied, "What's the most we want to pay?"

"We can't go over three hundred per night Reg," Yogi says, "anything over that and we will struggle to pay for the equipment and get your tax money back."

"Yeah I get the point, but it's so perfect."

The man to see to hire the football club hall was a chap called David Boggins. He owns a string of pubs and the football club. The main pub, where David lives, is in the Bennetts End area of Hemel where I was brought up. Bennetts End and Adeyfield were the first new areas to be built in Hemel Hempstead new town, so this is where the first batch of Londoners were moved out to, and they have still kept their values. Some of them are tough looking people but they are nice as pie really and look after their own, if you know what I mean. I call them the Mafia boys and some of them have certainly helped me out in the past whether I was being bullied or needed some quick cash or something being dealt with which was beyond my capabilities. Like one day, when someone owed me some money for some work I had done and was slow in paying me; it would get sorted. You know the type of people I'm trying to describe; lovely people who look after their own and thank God I was one of their own.

I said to Yogi and Chris, "We'll have to go and speak to David Boggins at the Cockerel" (the pub is called Greenacres Tavern now but I still know it as the Golden Cockerel).

Chris said, "Oh do we have to."

Yogi says, "I'll come with you if you want Reg, but I think you'll do better on your own as you know them all. You can have a quiet word with David Boggins, he might look after you on the price more than if the three of us went to see him."

"Okay, cheers, lads! I'll see what I can do."

So the very next day, about eleven thirty, I called in at the Golden Cockerel. David Boggins was sat at a table doing some paperwork.

"Can you spare a minute David?" I asked.

David looked up and in his Irish accent said, "Hello Reg son, how's your mum's cancer?"

"Oh she's really ill at the moment, she's up at St. Francis Hospice."

"Oh dear," David replied in a quiet voice. "Have a cup of coffee, what can I do for you son?"

"I wondered if I could hire your club house at the football ground about four times a year for a Northern Soul night." I went through the normal nightmare of trying to explain of what it was all about, but trying to explain about Northern Soul to someone who isn't into it is about as hard as finding an original copy of "Do I Love You (Indeed I Do)".

David said, "I'm not allowed discos any more, unless it's a charity event." Just as the look of disappointment was about to show on my face, he said, "So, what we will do is, you run the event the way you normally would, then I will donate some of the bar takings to where your Mum is (the St. Francis Hospice) and that way everyone is happy."

"Brilliant," I replied. "Now all I need to know is what it's gonna cost me."

"Well it's a three hundred plus venue Reggie but as you're the same as me, a Liverpool fan, it's going to cost you this much."

David wrote a figure on a piece of paper, I looked down at the price he had written and said, "I'll double that figure David."

"Whatever," David replied. "It's all going to your mum's hospice. The only thing you have to do for me is keep your mouth buttoned on what it's cost you."

So we shook hands on the deal. David said, "It's a pleasure doing business with you Reggie, you're a man after me own heart, let me know the dates you want to hire it and I will put them in the diary."

I won't tell you what the hall cost us because when the likes of these wonderful people tell you to keep your mouth shut, you keep your mouth shut. All I can say is that Yogi and Chris could not believe what David had done for us!

After arranging the dates around Chris's scooter weekends, my Caister Soul do's and trying not to clash with any of the events held locally, Chris and I went to the Cockerel to book and pay for the nights we wanted to hire the club. On our way to the pub, I started to wind Chris up by saying when we walk into the pub, if anyone says, "Hi Reg, what's you and your mate drinking, tell them what you want. Don't say 'No, I'm alright' and then go and buy one because they will get offended."

Chris put his hand on his forehead and said, "Oh no, really." He then looked over at me as I was trying not to laugh and said, "You little shit, stop winding me up."

All the Soul nights we've held at Hemel Football Club have been a huge success so far. As I'm writing this part of my book we have now held six Soul do's there. In four weeks time we will be holding our second anniversary and I've already sold seventy tickets. Straight after that the three of us will see David Boggins with next year's dates and take it from there.

The first night we held the Sounds Of Soul at Hemel FC the Soulies were overwhelmed by the venue and were well impressed with the bar so it looks like we've cracked it.

Peter Tebbutt who runs the Talk of the South Soul Club at Luton Rugby Club strolled over to me and said, "You lads have done it again. How do you keep finding these brilliant halls with magnificent dance floors? And this time it's got its own bar."

Yogi overheard Pete's conversation, put his hand on my shoulder and says, "That's it Reg, we've got five out of four right now, good parking, great dance floor, fantastic venue, lovely people attending and now brilliant bar facilities as well. As long as we keep the music right and they don't knock the place down, this is where we'll stay. What's your 'old Soul classic' tonight then?"

"It's going to be dedicated to all our kids Yogi,"

"Go on then, what is it?"

"'Be Young, Be Foolish And Be Happy' by The Tams".

"Brilliant," Yogi says, "I don't know how you get away with it, you'll be running out of them soon." He's not far wrong either. So far the 'old Soul classics' I finish my sets with in this order were:

If You Really Love Me	Stevie Wonder
Ain't No Mountain High Enough	Marvin and Tammi
Everything Is Tuesday	Chairman Of The Board
Walk In The Night	Junior Walker
Be Young Be Foolish Be Happy	The Tams
The Love I Lost	Harold Melvin
Dangling On A String	Chairman Of The Board
I Guess I'll Always Love You	Isley Brothers
I'm Going To Give Her All The Love I've Got	Jimmy Ruffin

On the second anniversary, I thought of starting with a slow record working my way up to a full crescendo and to finish with a 'choon', which is so fast, only the brilliant dancers will be able to cope with it.

The 'choon' might be 'Seven Rooms Of Gloom' by The Four Tops—this should sort the men out from the boys. So far the best 'old Soul classic' and the most talked about I've played has to be 'The Love I Lost' by Harold Melvin And The Blue Notes.

A week after that event, I was dancing at the Right Track in Peterborough and one of the Yarmouth crew called Mark Surridge comes over to me and says, "All the bloody way home from Hemel to Yarmouth we were singing 'The Love I Lost'. How can a tuppenny ha'penny record have such an impact on people that spend thousands of pounds on rare Soul? It was brilliant Reg, I loved it; well done."

Then three weeks later, Tim Brown played it at Luton. I reckon Steve Hagans (Emma's brother) must have told Tim the reaction it got when it was played at Hemel. (Well, that's what I'd like to think happened).

Chapter 27

Nothing Changes, Does It?

Over the last six years, it seems that quite a few of us old Northern Soul fans have been called back to this strange music cult. I don't know if there was anything like it anywhere else in the world, or will be ever again. Where teenagers from all over the country were called, via their mates or through reading Soul magazines, to certain venues hundreds of miles away from where they lived, just to listen and dance to these unknown Soul records. Most of them have the most saddest 'slit your wrists to' lyrics, then once they have got back home they couldn't wait for the next weekend so they could do it all again.

So it wasn't just a teenage fad, which we were going to grow out of because after a short lull and twenty-odd years later we are doing it all over again. I often wonder if we are refusing to grow up and get old or still believe this thing of ours is still so special, especially when you meet old friends and conversations carry on from where you left them all those years ago.

This kind of thing is happening to me all the time. Take for instance the last time I went to the 6 T's Mafia Soul Club at Plinston. On this particular occasion, I was completely knocked off my feet and reduced to tears. What a special night this turned out to be.

Yogi and I only went on the off chance, as we were attending our old mate Stan Brewster's fiftieth birthday party with my Mum, Dad and my brother Geoff. When Stan's party was in full swing at about 10.30pm me and Yogi said to Mum, Dad and Geoff, "We're gonna disappear now."

My Mum looked up and said, "I bet you pair of buggers are going Souling. Nothing changes does it son; have a good time, I'll see you in the morning."

Yogi and I arrived at Plinston around about 11.30pm. We both got on the floor straight away trying to make up for those lost hours of dancing. Opposite to where Yogi and I were, on the other side of the hall, my mate Dean Allport was dancing and a young girl kept bumping into him.

Another girl said to Dean, "Do you want me to have a word with her, it's not right her keep getting in your way like that I'll speak to her."

Dean replies, "It's alright. If it keeps happening I'll speak to her myself."

The girl replied, "I'll have a word if you like it's no trouble."

"No, you're okay," said Dean. "I'll sort it, what's your name?"

"I'm Janie from Worcester."

"I'm Dean from Hemel Hempstead."

"Did you say Hemel Hempstead? I went out with a smashing bloke from Hemel about twenty- five years ago."

"Did you," said Dean. "What was his name?"

"It was Reggie,"

"He's here," Dean says.

"No he wouldn't be here. There's no way it's the same person."

"Well we'll soon see," says Dean. "I'll take you over to him."

So there I was dancing away when I get a tap on my shoulder.

I said, "Alright Dean." Then I was just about to say, "Who's your lovely girlfriend?" when Janie said, "Hello Reg, Long time no see. You must have known like a bad penny I'd turn up one day."

Oh my God! I was speechless. We held each other for a few seconds then got all soppy and started booing, then when I did finally get to say something it was, "Oh Janie, I thought..."

"I know what you thought Reg, but here I am, still alive and kicking and I hope I've got a few years left in me yet. You see, I done what you said, I went back to my dad's and sorted myself out."

"But why has no one seen or heard of you? On numerous occasions I have asked about you and people have said, 'Forget it Reg you know how ill she was.' I don't understand it."

"Let's get off the dance floor Reg, we'll stand by the stage and I'll tell you all about it."

When we both got to the stage, Janie gave me a massive kiss then my other mate Jennie looked over and said, "What the hell is going on here? One minute they're crying then the next minute they're snogging! Who the hell is she? I've never seen her before."

Then Kay Seabrook says to Jen, "I don't know who the girl is. You'll have to go and ask him."

Jennie's reply was "I will when she let's go of him. Any more of that and I'll tell his wife."

Kay replied, "Give the boy a chance to explain; you're not his bloody mother Jen."

Within half an hour Janie had told me her story.

"You see Reg after 'the Casino' shut, I emigrated to Australia, got married and had two kids. I've also done quite well in business, so everything was fine till my husband got off with one of my neighbours at one of my own barbecues. Now I've come back to England to find to my amazement that the Northern Soul scene is stronger now than it was before I left. But this is the icing on the cake, who would have thought after all these years."

"Yeah, I know what you mean Sister, what's your favourite sound at the moment Janie?"

"It's got to be 'Independent Woman' by Jan Jones, it's the story of my life at the moment Reg. What's yours?"

"'I Need Love' by Daybreak."

"Ah, great sound Reg, nothing changes does it?"

"Not really Janie, give us your phone number and I'll let you know when our next Sounds Of Soul do is on and hopefully you'll be able to come and meet my family.

Another time this kind of thing happened to me was when Chris and Yogi took me to the Stoke all-nighter at the Kings Hall. Chris desperately wanted me to see the place, and I must admit it was the nearest to the feeling I had to when I went to Wigan Casino, since coming back to the Northern Soul scene.

The things I liked were queuing up to get in which was a bit nostalgic, then once inside the high ceiling was magnificent—Wedgwood blue and white painted mouldings with a cambered shape, looking something like the roof at Lime Street station in Liverpool. Also, the dance floor was real wood and the place had a balcony as well. Another thing I noticed was how clean it all was.

After a few minutes of taking it all in, Chris came over to me and says, "What do you think Reg? Is it like Wigan?"

It was when Chris said, "Is it better than Wigan Casino?"

I stopped taking in what I was seeing and said, "What do you think? Is this the best venue you go to at the moment?"

Chris replied, "Oh yes."

"Well then. If you like, this is your Wigan. This is your favourite place you go to but all the other smaller clubs should not to be ignored. Now your other question, 'Is it like Wigan Casino?' The difference is my Wigan was open every Saturday night, yours is four or five times a year at the most. The other differences are when I was in my Wigan it was like you were dancing in a red-hot furnace. The place stank of sweat and stale Brut aftershave. It was a scruffy place with bits of plaster and nicotine droplets falling from the ceiling. If you sat and watched the feet of the dancers moving you would see small clouds of talcum powder bouncing off the sprung loaded floor. Then of course, there were the famous toilets. You couldn't go and get changed in a civilised manner like you do in your Wigan; a nice little wash and brush up and lay your new set of clothing out whilst changing—it would be impossible to get changed like that in my Wigan. The toilets stank when you walked in and you had to hold your trousers up by your knees to save the pee water rising up your Wigan breeches. If you weren't on tiptoe, you would definitely get your socks wet, which in turn caused blisters through dancing which could turn septic from the pee. I always got changed in a dark corner near where we were sitting.

"So, is your Wigan better than mine? No chance. If I was you, what I suggest you do is every time you visit this wonderful place, take time to look around and savour every minute, take some pictures and enjoy it while it lasts just in case someone takes away your most favourite place like they did mine."

Then our conversation was broken up when Yogi said, "What do you think of the place Reg?"

"Same as you Yogi, it's wonderful isn't it?"

"Come with me Reg, I've got someone I want you to meet."

We walked out of the main ballroom, up some stairs where there was a bar, which was situated quite close to the modern room.

Yogi and I entered the bar and Yogi says, "There you go Reg, the chap sitting at that table with the record box."

I look over and the chap says in a Bradford accent, "Hello Reg, still like that focking Carstairs record? It's focking shite."

As soon as the chap said these words, I knew instantly it was Steve from Bradford, "Of course I do Steve, it's still one of me favourites."

"Oh focking hell. Nothing changes does it?"

I wasn't surprised that Steve remembered after all those years because when we were kids Steve used to introduce us to his mates by saying, "This is Yogi and Reg from London and Reg only likes the focking Carstairs." Then one of Steve's friends would say, "Well these Londoners haven't got much idea yet, have they mate?"

Yogi and I sat chatting with Steve for about an hour. I asked him where Maggie was and he informed me that they had had a divorce "but I still see her now and then". He said, "I'll tell her that I've seen you, she will be pleased to know that you are still about and still dancing as well, she will be impressed."

During our conversation, Chris joined just to sit and listen to us all talking about those magic times we used to have. Then I shook Steve's hand and said, "I've got to go now mate, the dance floor is calling."

Steve's reply was, "I know exactly what you mean mate, you go and enjoy yourself Reg and I'll see you about."

Chapter 28

Joy and Pain

It's 2005 and everything is going sweet. Our Sounds Of Soul club is better than Chris, Yogi and I could ever have imagined. Due to us lending our disco equipment to a new Soul club in our area called Blue Skies, Yogi and Chris had been asked to DJ for them. DJing outside of our own Soul club is very uplifting for us all because when someone asks if you will be interested in DJing for their Soul club, it's proof that we can't be going far wrong with the music that we play at our own, so everything is good. As for yours truly, on a personal note, it appeared that I was easing myself out of the debts that occurred in the past when things out of the norm were happening to my family and me.

I'd also been given another scooter by one of my mates, Paul Tooley. It was a rusty as hell Lamberetta LD 1958, the same year as my Vespa so I will seek Chris's advice and have a go at restoring it. I've seen a LD recently, which has been restored and it's bloody beautiful. It's called Peaches and Cream. If things go to plan my LD will be Coffee and Cream and I'm going to call my new scooter Café Latte. Paul couldn't have given me the scooter at a better time, as at this time in my life, I really needed to be occupied.

The reason for this was my Mum. Mum's illness was getting worse and I didn't know what to do. Everything else I'm involved in I feel I have under control, but when it comes to someone you love who is dying, you feel helpless. Even when lovely people who care about you so much surround you, you still have tendencies to feel so lonely. Also being a dad, when these circumstances arise, you try and be strong for the rest of your family and I feel that I can't seek advice and comfort from the people that I'm trying to give it to. As for my best mate Yogi, he was probably feeling the same pain that I was. You see my mum was a mum to most of my mates as well. At one time or another, they would all ask her advice on things however trivial they might have been. Her classic answer, whoever it was, would be, "Don't worry, you'll be alright, it will all come out in the wash. If you need any money or anything let me know and we will try and sort it out." You might say my Mum was a mum of the people, which makes me extremely proud of her.

As I work for myself, I was able to get to the hospice anytime I wanted to during the week. I would go early in the mornings and try and get her to eat something before my sister and Dad arrived, but on Fridays I would go in the afternoon, just before I got ready to go Souling or sort the disco equipment out.

Around this time Yogi had taken some bookings for our disco, we had a couple of birthdays and a wedding. On the Saturdays, Mum's last words to me would be, "Keep dancing Son and if anyone has booked your disco, don't let them down. Do a good job however ill I get, you can tell me all about it the next morning."

I thought, "Yeah all right Mum, that's easier said than done, ain't it." So although I was busy I was pretty worried. One minute I was on a massive high whilst DJing and making people happy and as soon as the night finished I was slumping into a very low mode and felt a touch of despair. Talk about 'Messing With Your Mind'.

During this topsy-turvy time of my life, the advice and comfort I was seeking came from one of the most unlikely sources, a girl who I hardly knew called Karen Bedford. Once again it was a night when Yogi and I were Souling at Plinston. We were dancing in the main hall and I said to Yogi, "I'm going into the Modern room for half an hour."

Yogi laughed and said, "I'll see you when it's finished then, I know what you're like once you get in that Modern room."

I must admit, I do like the modern sounds it makes a nice change. Although I love all the oldies I just can't get my head around the R&B sounds, so when a DJ is an R&B specialist I'm inclined to disappear into the Modern room, especially if it's a time when one of my favourite DJs called Taffy Guy is playing. I put Taffy in my top five DJs at this present time and some of my favourite 'choons' that Taffy has been playing recently are: 'My Good Friend James' by The Pioneers; 'Something For My Head' by Bobby Womack; 'What Does It Take To Win Your Love' The Electrifying Cashmeres; 'I Think You're Wonderful' by Aretha Franklin; 'Where Do You Go When The Party Is Over?' Archie Bell and The Drells.

And so on.

I must say I really like listening to Taffy's sets, the music is second to none. The only down side is it's so expensive to listen to him play his set because when Taffy has finished his hour's play, you're wondering where the hell you're going to get the money to buy the next half a dozen new sounds on your 'wants list'. Listening to Taffy's idea of Soul music is brilliant, but be prepared to spend some money if you're an avid vinyl collector.

On this particular occasion when I entered the Modern room, I could see Karen was really upset. As I walked over to where she was sitting, one of the top dancers called Chantal grabbed my arm and said, "You're just the man I'm looking for Reg. Will you sit with Karen for me? She's having a bit of a bad time of it at the moment. If anyone can cheer her up, it would be you."

I said to Chantal, "I'll give it a go but don't be long. I'm not having it easy myself at the moment."

Chantal's reply was, "I know you're not mate but we're all here for you. See what you can do, I won't be long."

So I go and sit next to Karen, put my arm around her shoulder and ask, "Are you alright?"

Her answer was, "No I fuckin' ain't! Don't waste your time with me Reg. No one can help me the state I'm in; go and have a dance."

My reply was, "Sorry mate can't do that. You've set the challenge now and I like a challenge. Did I detect a small grin there?"

"No you didn't."

Although this was a very difficult conversation, to my amazement it was going to be the start of one of those very special friendships we've all witnessed at one time or another being involved with Soul music. Rather than doing as Chantal had requested to help Karen, I found through listening to what Karen had to say our conversations were making me feel a lot better about the nightmare I was going through. You see Karen had been through a similar situation two years previously when she lost someone she loved. In her case it was Randy Cousens (her boyfriend). After talking to various Soulies and to Karen about Randy, I came to the conclusion this was a man I really wished I'd met, but unfortunately Randy had passed away before I had the privilege. Everyone I spoke to about Randy said he was one in a million, a great bloke. Karen reckons I would have got on great with Randy as we had similar views on the music. There were no airs or graces about the man, just a hard working fella who loved the music and the people around him. Although we never met, through talking to other people, I really feel we had.

So, God bless you mate. When it's my turn to walk on that big dance floor in the sky, look out for a little bald bloke with a massive smile and that will be me. 'I can't wait.'

The following week Chris phoned Yogi and me to inform us that it was the week of our friend Brian Coleman's wedding. Chris also reminded me that it's the week of our scooter club too, he then said, "but if you're not there we'll all understand, your main priority is to look after your Mum."

"I expect I'll be there, as being so busy helps me to cope with it all, plus when I go and see my Mum she wants to know how whatever we were doing went and who was there. She likes to know what's going on outside the hospice and how were all doing. She doesn't seem to like talking about herself. The only time she does talk about things in the hospice is when something funny has happened."

Chris's reply was, "She's brilliant Reg. You get there when you can. Brian is fetching his list of music he wants played, but if you're not there don't worry, I will deal with it. Look after yourself and don't wear yourself out. Is Karen looking after you?"

"Yes she is, I'm thinking of taking her to meet Mum."

"And how's Debbie, Jack and Holly coping?"

"We're all getting tired but we're all alright."

"Okay Reg, let me know if anything happens I'll see you in the week."

On the following Wednesday I did manage to get to the scooter club but it was only for the last hour. As soon as I walked in the Unicorn pub where our scooter club is held, Brian and Chris strolled over.

Brian said, "All the music is sorted Reg, Chris has got my list and the main record me and my wife want to dance to is 'Tonight Is The Night' by Betty Wright. Now how's your mum?"

"Not good at the moment Bri. One minute the doctor's saying she's only got hours and the next she looks great—talk about 'Messing With Your Mind'".

"I really feel for you Reg," Brian replied. "I obviously want you at my wedding but please don't worry if you can't make it. Wish your mum all the best, keep your chin up Son and hopefully I will see you on Saturday night."

During the next couple of days, Mum kept slipping in and out of consciousness. Although I was very doubtful about attending Brian's wedding in between visiting Mum, I sorted out the records that Brian had asked for to the best of my ability.

On the Saturday morning when I arrived at the hospice, Mum still appeared out of it so I quietly sat by her bed. I had just taken a sip of tea when all of a sudden I hear, "Hello Son!" Well, my tea shot up in the air.

"You frightened the bloody life out of me, Mother, it's nice to have you back."

"What day is it, Son?"

"Saturday the 11th Mum."

"You're going to a wedding today aren't you?"

"It looks like I am Mother, hang on a minute I'll give Jackie a ring."

"Hello Jack, Mum's come back to life again."

Jackie my sister replied, "Oh that's good, I'll tell Dad and Geoff. Stay with Mum till I get there, I won't be long, then you can go to your wedding. I'll stay with Mum tonight. See you soon."

I sat with Mum talking, we spoke about the usual things, the weather, how long Mum had been asleep, dad, Jackie and Geoff, Brian's wedding. When my dad and sister arrived I said, "I'm off now Mum."

Her words were getting to be a routine now. "Okay Son, do a good job, have a good time and I'll see you in the morning you can tell me all about it."

When I walked into Brian's wedding carrying my record box, Brian was right in the middle of his speech. Then whilst Chris, Yogi and I were playing some background music, Brian strolled over all suited and booted and says, "Reg, you're here. What's happened? How's your mum?"

"Well," I said, "Mum's come back to life again she was sitting up talking about your wedding, I can't believe it. This is the third time this has happened."

Brian's reply was, "Bless her, you give her my love when you see her."

"Right," I said, "Let's get this wedding rolling."

Chris and I started the evening with some 'old Soul classics' (Youth Club music). Then Yogi played a blinder of a set. I don't know how he does it every time. He's the only guy who can fill the floor even when he plays a crap record like 'I Love To Love' by Tina Charles, the man's been cracking me up all my life and still continues to do so.

Then it was my turn again and I played most of Brian's list with some Jazz, Funk and Club music: 'Dominoes' by Donald Byrd; 'Just Can't Give You Up' by Mystic Merlin; 'Daylight' Bobby Womack etc.

Then came the highlight of the evening, when Chris played some Garage and House music and to my amazement he even knew all the dance steps as well. He was putting the records on and as soon as they kicked in he was away in his own little world doing the fish tank dance, big box little box etc. The whole affair was 'I want your autograph' material.

On the Sunday I got to the hospice early and Mum was still with us, her first words were, "Hello Son, how did it go then?"

"Well Mum, most of Brian's guests said we were brilliant."

"Aah, you say that all the time, your discos can't be that good every time."

Just as Mum had spoken, Brian sent me a text message from his honeymoon suite saying how brilliant he thought it was. I passed Mum the mobile and said, "We've had a text Mum."

She read the message and says, "Bloody hell, another happy customer, well done Son."

Chapter 29

Saying Goodbye to Mother

It's late November 2005 and Christmas is approaching. Things are looking a little bit brighter. Mum is still in the Hospice and conscious most of the time; her energy levels are a lot higher and her conversations are now lasting about fifteen minutes, so under the circumstances we're doing all right. Around this time of the year I start to get pretty busy teaching people to ski, in this case four of my friends: Malcolm Apted, who obviously needs to keep pretty busy after losing his wife Tracy to the dreaded cancer, Dave White, Simon Jessop and his daughter Amber. I'm having some great evenings with this little group of skiers and if I can possibly pass the ski exam I've been waiting to pass for about five years, I will ask this small group if they would like to come away with me to the French Alps next season because if things go well by then I will be a qualified Alpine ski leader.

It was on one of these evenings where Karen Bedford my newfound Soul mate met me at the Hemel Hempstead ski centre and we went to visit mother. I suppose this was a small gamble on my behalf, taking Karen to visit another cancer patient. Karen was still struggling to get her head around the loss of Randy but the gamble paid off, because Karen appears to have a better acceptance of some of the shit life throws at us all now and then. I wanted to try and give something back for the help I was receiving from knowing her. Through knowing Karen, I was always kept busy on the Soul scene and didn't realise the number of small soul do's going on locally. Around this time I had to pick and choose the do's I was attending, as there was no way I wanted to be more than an hour away. So I was only Souling with Yogi when the travelling met this criteria: if I was only an hour away from the hospice, I felt that I could get there in time if anything happened to Mum.

This is where Karen came into her own. I got a phone call on the Tuesday night in one of the weeks leading up to Christmas saying, "Right Reg, I made a small list of all the Soul do's coming up. The first is at the Hatfield Social Club, which will be good as it's only twenty minutes away. The music is Jazz Funk, a little bit of Northern, and Ady Potts is playing, plus it's only three pounds to get in so if you're up for it I'll pick you up. Also there is a small do at Bar 12 opposite the Galleria in a couple of weeks, we'll have to play it by ear Reg, depending on how your Mum is. I've sorted out about three or four and they're all less than an hour away."

You certainly realise what people mean to you in your hours of need and I'm happy to say that through Karen's actions and thoughtfulness, I managed to get to all of the Soul do's that she had mentioned.

The first at Hatfield Social club was a blinding little night. Karen arranged to pick me up at eight o'clock. When she arrived, she wasn't in her own car as she got one of her mates Geoff Green to drive instead. Geoff was a slightly older chap than me and seemed to like a few of the same sounds I liked, a couple mentioned in our small conversation whilst travelling to Hatfield were 'These Memories' by Almetta Lattimore and 'My Good Friend James' by The Pioneers. In my opinion, both are top tunes at the moment.

It was only when I entered this venue, I realised that Christmas was nearly upon us; this small working men's club was well spruced up with lots of Crimbo decorations. There was a small wooden dance floor and the place was quite busy with everyday type disco goers. Then we saw Ady Potts, his wife Sue and Graham Driver, who runs the Soul club at Hitchin Town football club at a table by the dance floor so Karen, Geoff and myself made our way over to where they were sitting.

I quite like going to these small Soul do's as you seem to have a lot more time to talk and meet people. Talking to Ady, he told me that he was going to play more of the funky type 'choons' when it was his turn to DJ. This was new to me as I didn't know he owned any of this type of music.

Ady also asked if there was a sound he could play for me.

"Yes," I said, "Have you got your copy of 'I Need Love' by Daybreak with you?"

"Of course I have, it's in the box. I'll play that sound for you Reg. Let's have a look. Here you go!"

Ady passed me the record. I got that instant buzz you get when avid record collectors like us are just holding a rare gem, let alone owning one. I held it as if it was bone china then looked at the label; it was on an orange PAP. I asked Ady what kind of money we are talking about for a sound like this?

Ady replied, "Anything between £500 to £800." At that moment, I carefully handed the record back so Ady could put it safely in his record box. Three weeks later, the record was repressed on an orange PAP for £5 a copy, but in my eyes this didn't devalue Ady's mint copy of the original.

This little Soul night with Geoff and Karen was really a top night out; nice venue, great company and everyone in the Christmas spirit. The following week was the Soul do at Bar 12. I arranged to meet Karen at the Galleria shopping centre by the Macdonald's burger bar. From where I was standing, I could see Bar 12 on the other side of the dual carriageway. The small venue was painted white with a fluorescent blue Bar 12 sign advertising the place. When we eventually walked across the busy road and entered the place, it was like a posh little wine bar with light wooden tables that I think were made of ash.

All down the side of one wall was the bar—quite a grand looking bar, a typical wine bar with a coffee machine, you know the type? At one end of the bar was a small alcove roughly about twenty feet by ten feet, which was allocated for dancing. Also in this alcove was the disco stand, the dance floor had a quarry tiled surface and to my amazement was quite good to dance on. Whilst Karen was getting some drinks and chatting, like most of the female of the species devote their lives to doing, I took a stroll towards where the disco was set up as you couldn't see who was playing from where I was standing. I suppose in this instance it was similar to the old Catacombs in Wolverhampton where you could hear the 'choons' but couldn't see where they were coming from. When I finally reached the disco stand the DJ was Ady Potts.

He looked up and said, "Cor blimey, I don't see you for ages Reg, then I see you two weeks running!"

"Well," I said, "I've only popped in to see if you're ready to sell your copy of 'I Need Love' for a fiver."

"Yes alright Reg. Add another £600 and I might consider it. How's your Mum?"

"She seems okay at the moment, touch wood, we're gonna see if the hospice will let her out for Christmas."

Ady's reply was, "Ah good luck on that one Reg, that will be great mate."

I strolled back to where Karen was with my drink and she was still jawing to her mate Chrissie, then in walked my mate Kev Matthews with one of his friends. So that made about fifteen of us, and that was as busy as the night was gonna get. Although there weren't many Soulies there, this do turned out to be another blinding little night and the icing on the cake was when Martin Ainscough walked over to where I was sitting and said, "Just the man I wanted to see, Reg."

"Really what have I done?"

"Nothing yet; it's what I want you to do. You know when I borrowed the Sounds Of Soul disco equipment?"

"Yep, what you wanna borrow it again?"

"No I've already let Yogi and Chris DJ at one of my dos and now it's your turn, but this is a special do as it's my birthday. It's on the 30th January and you'll be lining up with Mac from Soul in the City, John Stubbs and Geoff Green."

"Geoff Green—I was out with him last week."

"Oh, and I forgot to mention Arthur Fenn."

"Arthur Fenn, you're joking me! He's one of me favourites, and you want me. Martin you're the first person that has asked me to DJ outside of Sounds Of Soul. I feel highly honoured, but…"

"I know what you're gonna say Reg, so rather than me get someone else in, if your Mum takes a turn for the worse I'll stand in for you myself so if something does happen I don't want you to think you're letting me down."

"Bloody hell, thanks very much Martin what would you like me to play?"

"Well Arthur will be playing modern, Mac is playing some rare R&B so a nice mixture wouldn't go a miss, some oldies, newies, you can even throw in some of your Caister teapot sounds if you like, as it's my birthday."

"Thanks Martin, I'll keep in touch and let you know how things are going, I can't wait."

After speaking with Martin, I catch Karen's attention as she is still jawing away with Chrissie. I nod in a fashion that I want her to meet me at the bar. I order us both a drink, then Karen strolls over to me and asks, "What's up?"

I passed Karen her drink and said, "You'll never guess, Martin Ainscough has only asked me to DJ at the next Blue Skies Soul night and I'm lining up along side the likes of Arthur Fenn."

"Good it's about time, you must be pleased with that Reg. I bet Arthur's a bit worried."

"Yeah, right sister, I'd cut off me right arm just to own one of Arthur's records from his box, he's one of the best and you know it."

"You'll be all right Reg, I've got every faith in you." Our conversation was broken up by the sound of 'The Game Is Over' by Brown Sugar. Without saying a word, we both headed for the dance floor. The next 'choon' was 'Too Late' by Mandrill, followed by 'I Need Love' by Daybreak. We both ended up staying on the floor until the night was finished. Another brilliant night, only twenty minutes away from where I lived.

In the following weeks leading up to Christmas, my family had a meeting with Roz Taylor, the doctor in charge at the hospice. After agreeing with our family wishes, it was 'Operation Get Mum Home For Christmas'. Roz Taylor organised all the equipment we were going to need; electric bed, wheelchair, oxygen etc.

On the night we finally got Mum home, it happened to be the Christmas shopping night for wheelchairs in Hemel town centre.

When Mum arrived home her first words were, "We're all going shopping aren't we?"

Well, she looked so ill and breathless we said, "Is that really what you want to do Mum?"

Her reply was, "Oh yes." So we loaded up my car with everything we thought we needed, gave mum a quick puff of oxygen then off we went.

When we arrived at the car park in Hemel town, everything we had to do to make Mum comfortable seemed to take ages. Once my Dad, sister, brother Geoff and I finally got her in her wheelchair all wrapped up in blankets, we gave her a couple of puffs from the oxygen bottle and off we set. Whist walking around the town with my brother, sister, Mum and Dad, the thoughts that came into my mind was of that sad bit in the film *Last Snows of Spring*, where the dad had got the owner of the fairground to open every ride at about five o'clock in the morning so his son, who was seriously ill could have some last precious moments sitting in a swan fairground ride with his dad. That's what we all appeared to be doing with mother, but in her case her favourite pastime was shopping.

As we went pass the Ann Summers sex shop, the staff were enticing people through the door by offering them a free glass of sherry, wine or mince pies, so in we all go! Mum was peeing herself laughing at some of the items being sold. After that we pushed her down to Marks and Spencers, where a choir was singing 'Silent Night'. I don't know if this is a hard to come by tune on a rare record label, but the live version was just perfect. When the song they were singing finished, there was a small frenzy occurring within the members of the choir, as some of them were carers from Mum's Hospice. A quite warm feeling came over me when I heard one of them say to her mate. "The Stickings family have only brought Colleen Christmas shopping! Whatever will they do next?"

When my Dad and I finally got Mum in my car after another couple of puffs of oxygen, I announced that I had one more thing to do. I asked Mum if she was up for a surprise and her reply was, "I am if I don't have to get out of the car. Getting in and out of the car is killing me."

"Okay Mother," I replied, and then I drove down the lower Nash Mills road to a house smothered in the most amazing Christmas decorations.

I pulled up outside and said to Mum, "What do you think of that then?"

Her reply was, "Bloody lovely Son"

Then I said, "I won't be a minute."

Leaving Mum and Dad in the car, I walked up the path and knocked on the front door of the house. When the owner answered the door, he was dressed in a full Father Christmas outfit. I quickly explained the situation and he looked at me with a massive smile, winks and says, "Leave it to me Son."

As this chap walked towards my Mum and Dad in the car, halfway down his garden path he flicked a switch and said, "It's gonna take about five minutes to warm up."

I didn't have a clue what he was going on about, but when he arrived at the car, my Mum undid the window. The chap wished her well and said. "What would you like for Christmas then?"

"A new life wouldn't go a miss," said Mum, "but as that's not going to happen, I'd like it to snow for Christmas."

"Well you'd better look in my garden then," and as we all looked back in the chap's garden, it was snowing hard. The switch he flicked was only for his bloody snow machine, wasn't it!

Mum looked at the chap with a tear in her eye and said, "Thanks very much mate."

This night was to be the start of a very special Christmas. My Mum got to spend a day with each one of her three kids, it was my house Christmas Eve, Jackie's Christmas Day, but on Boxing Day, Mum was too tired to get to Geoff's so he went to her house.

On Christmas Day, Mum gave me a black plastic bag and said, "Here's your present from me and Dad."

Inside were the two Lambretta seats for the LD I'm doing up. They had been re-upholstered in Beige and Cream leatherette and had been sown in an oyster shell-stitching pattern, just as requested.

"Cheers Mum."

Then the strangest thing happened on the Boxing Day. I spent the day with Jenny Knight and some friends, Michelle Bennett and Bobby Garland. We had a brilliant time as usual. Jenny cooked dinner, which consisted of a massive piece of 'boilly' bacon, which she had cooked with spiky cloves stuck in the outside skin; all professional like. After lunch, Jenny and I started playing our records, both trying to out do each other. I must say Jenny's got some brilliant sounds but I won in the end. I played 'Too Late' by Mandrill.

As soon as the record kicked in Jenny says, "That's it. I'm not playing any more, you're not allowed to play records of that quality on my stereo."

"Have I won then, Jen?"

"Yes of course you have. Put it on again, you know it's one of my favourites, you little sod."

Around about nine o'clock when all the others had gone home, Jenny and I finished off the last of the After Eight mints then I said, "I'm gonna call it a day."

Jenny replies, "Well I've made your bed up, what time do you want me to wake you?"

"About seven thirty Jen, I've got to work at the ski centre tomorrow, I've got to repair a broken window."

"Okay," Jen replied. "I'll set the alarm for seven thirty."

At seven thirty the following day Jenny comes into my room and says, "Reg you'll never guess, I reckon your Mum's had a word with the big man upstairs, look out of the window."

When I drew the curtains and looked outside, everywhere was white and it was snowing hard. I thought to myself 'well Mother that's the icing on the cake ain't it? Your last Christmas has been the best ever!'

The following week, Mum had to go back to the Hospice and this is the worst I'd seen her. We probably overdid it during Christmas but Mum wouldn't have had it any different. You might say we gave it "full welly".

During the next couple of days, I got a phone call from my mate, Marcus Bell who runs a Modern Soul Club with his mate called Dave Blow. The Soul Club is called Treacle Soul—if you are a born and bred Hemelite you would know that this is a brilliant name for a Soul Club in Hemel as the old yokels used to call Hemel Hempstead, Treacle Bumpstead—hence the name Treacle Soul.

The phone call went, "Hi Reg how's your Mum? I've been thinking how you all coped over Christmas."

"Well Marcus, Mum's not good but our Christmas has been brilliant; we sort of treasured every moment."

Marcus then said, "After what you've just said, I've got something for you. Are you in for a while?"

"Yeah, I'm just sitting here mate."

"Okay, I'll see you in a minute."

When Marcus arrived at my house he passed me an LP and said "Put it on side two, track one."

So I started playing the sound and it's absolutely brilliant. When the record reached the chorus, the lyrics were '*I'll treasure the moment, those sweet moments, I spent with you.*' I say to Marcus, "Wow it's brilliant! Where could I get a copy of this?"

His reply was, "It's yours. I want you to have it to remind you of your Mum."

All the time this kind of thing happens to me, it underlines my belief in just how special these Soul people are, they really are the best people in the world.

In no time at all, it was Friday the thirteenth of Jan, the night I'd been waiting for a chance to play my idea of Soul music for someone else's Soul Club—Martin Ainscough's Blue Skies. I woke up about six thirty am, went downstairs and laid out my record set on the carpet. I chose about twenty records, approximately an hour's playing time. Then I started complaining of stomachache.

My wife Debbie said, "Calm down, you always get like this, it's excitement and nerves at the same time, take it easy go and see your Mum she will soon tell you."

"Okay," I replied. "I'll leave these records on the table 'cos I want to sort them into some type of playing order. Right I'll go and see my Mum then."

When I arrived at the Hospice, Mum can hardly speak, so I got up close to her and did most of the talking, I softly said, "Mum, tonight's the night I'm DJing alongside one of the best, Arthur Fenn. I know what you're going to say Mum, 'Do your best, enjoy yourself and don't let anyone down'."

Mum opened her eyes and whispered with a smile, "You don't 'arf make me laugh Son"

With that I had a little boo and went and got a cup of tea. When my sister Jackie arrived, I asked her, "What shall I do?"

Jackie's reply was, "There's nothing you can do Reg. What I would do if I was you is pick some of your closest friends and leave their mobile numbers so we can contact you if anything happens."

"Okay, that's what I will do, if Mum wakes up tell her I'll tell her all about it in the morning."

Then my sister says, "Go on then, don't cock it up, do your best and all that palarver."

"Okay sis, I'll see you in the morning."

So just before Yogi was about to pick me up and take me to the do I make a list of six friends' mobile numbers, they were: Yogi, Jenny, Kay, Chris, Lorraine and Karen. I said to all six friends if they get a phone call whilst I'm DJing wait till I finish playing my set and don't make a fuss. When my turn arrived to play I walked over to the stage with my small record box and a couple of LPs under my arm, but everything seemed different. I felt as cool as a cucumber and not one butterfly in me stomach. I kick off my set with 'She'll Come Running Back' by Mel Britt. Then the sounds to follow were:

Hey	Barbara Mercer
Overdose Of Joy	Eugene Record
Glow Love	Brook Benton
Treasure The Moment	The Pioneers
It Really Hurts Me Girl	The Carstairs
Colour Him Father	O. C. Smith
Pyramid	Soul Brothers Inc.
I Need Love	Daybreak.

Then I thanked all the Soulies who had texted me concerning my Mum and said, "So we'll play her record—'Praying' by Harold Melvin And The Blue Notes"

As usual, the Soulies danced their hearts out and then I played 'Come Get To This' by Marvin Gaye and 'You Don't Love Me' by Moses Smith. I followed on with a couple of others that I can't remember, and finished with an 'old soul classic', 'You've Got Me Dangling On A String'—Chairman Of The Board.

At the end of my set, most of the Soulies gave me a clap and a cheer and as I walked down the steps from the stage Jon Buck said, "That's the best I've ever heard you play Reg."

I replied, "Cheers Jon, I'll tell Mum you said that."

"Yeah, you tell her and give her my love."

On the Saturday, I got to the Hospice early to let Mum know how I got on but she was out of it, just lying there, breathing heavily with her mouth wide open. I didn't stay long, I didn't like seeing her like that. Then I went to see her on the Sunday after watching my son Jack play football, it was around about four o'clock in the afternoon.

When I arrived at the Hospice, Jackie was sitting with Mum but there was no change. I asked Jackie how she was; she said she was okay. I could see she was absolutely shattered and I asked her who was looking after Mum overnight, Jackie replied, "I am, I'm looking after her tonight."

I looked over to Mum and said, "They don't trust me, Mum."

Then after about twenty minutes of thinking my sister said, "If you want to look after her tonight you can, but if anything happens to her God help you."

I looked at Mum, feeling slightly under pressure, and said, "It looks like we've got ourselves an all-nighter, Mum. I'll have to nip home, get some bits and let Debbie know. Will you stay here till I get back Jack?"

Her reply was, "Of course I will, you twit. I'm not going anywhere am I?"

When I returned to the Hospice, I walked in carrying a bag with about eighty records, eighty cardboard covers, some coloured pens, three tins of Red Bull and this story that I'm trying to write. The reason for this was most times when I went to visit Mum, rather than just sitting there, we did things together, and I had to be as sharp as a razor on this particular occasion.

Once my sister had gone home, Mum and I got settled. I started the night by trying to write my book, but having no one to ask the spellings I felt about as much use as a chocolate teapot. So we watched telly for a while and approximately every twenty minutes I mopped Mum's brow and moistened her mouth with a cotton wool bud from a glass of water.

It was about 2am when the nurse said, "Why don't you have a sleep?"

"I'm not allowed," I replied. "My sister would kill me if something happens to Mum."

"Okay," said the nurse. "Whatever suits you. Is that records in that bag?"

"Yes," I replied.

"Are you pricing them up for a car boot sale? I reckon you would get about 10p each for them."

I placed three pieces of vinyl in the nurse's hand and informed her that she was holding about one and a half grand's worth.

"Oh my God," she said. "Take them back, so how much is in that old carrier bag then?"

"A few bobs' worth," I replied.

"Why have you bought them here?"

"Well," I said, "whenever I've been visiting Mum we would try to forget what's happening and do small jobs. Recently we've cut cherries for a cake, greased baking tins, sorted out some upholstery on a pair of Lambretta seats and tonight we're going to mark up some new cardboard covers for some records that haven't been done yet."

Then the nurse said, "Well that will be a job worth doing if the records are as dear as you say they are. We'll leave the small light on so you can work. See you in the morning."

As soon as the nurses left, I placed the eighty sounds on Mum's bed, then one by one I started copying the record titles onto the covers. Then if you snip the paper sleeve to size, both the record and the paper sleeve will fit in the cardboard cover. After I had about ten finished, I sensed that something was wrong. I looked towards Mum and thought she had stopped breathing. I carefully removed my records from her bed, walked around to where the electric apparatus was, which made the pillow end of the bed rise and fall and gave it a sudden jerk and with a groan Mum started breathing again.

"You can't do this to me Mum, if something happens to you tonight Jackie is going to go 'garratty'. You must hold on."

During the night this happened three times. On the third time, when I was about to leave Mum's side and find the nurses, I noticed that a ray of sunshine had started to filter through the curtains just like it used to when we were attending an all-nighter at Wigan Casino. Then within a few minutes, in walked my sister saying, "Well, how has she been then?"

"Fine," I said. "There's no change, she still looks like a zombie but I think she's comfortable."

"I see you managed to mark up all the record covers then."

"Yeah, Mum did half of them."

"No she didn't, the writing would have been a lot better than that if she had done them."

"Yeah I know Sis, I'm gonna go home now but I'm not going to work, I'll try and get my head down on the settee and I'll see you later."

Around about quarter to twelve I got a phone call from my brother's wife Lynn saying "They reckon it's not going to be long now, we're all here."

"Okay," I replied, "I'm not going to rush back. I'll take my time I'll see you soon."

Then fifteen minutes later Lynn phoned me back to tell me that Mum had passed away at twelve o'clock. The date was Monday 16th January 2006. I sent a text message to my mates on the *Soul Scene* saying, "My ordeal is finally over, Mum has just passed away, thank you for all your support. I love you all, Reg"

Within an hour I had received twenty-two replies from all you wonderful Soulies. This is when I realised what Mum meant when my sister said to her, "I don't know what Reggie's gonna do when you're not here anymore Mum. He appears to keep himself to himself."

Mum's reply was, "He'll be all right Jackie. He's got family all over England." And you know what, she was absolutely right. Being a member of this thing of ours is very special and always will be.

Around about three o'clock, I went around to Yogi's house, picked up Lorraine and we went out to dinner to celebrate Mum's life. It seemed the right thing to do! And I couldn't have picked a better person to share it with me.

Chapter 30

Life Couldn't Be Richer

After Mum had passed away, the rest of January 2006 seemed to take a sudden slump work-wise. I don't know if it was because the regulars I make things for felt that they shouldn't bother me or if there was a slump generally in the building trade. All I knew was that I was scratching around for work. Then whilst I was attending the Talk Of The South soul do in Luton, I happened to mention to my old mate Paul Tooley that I was a bit quiet on the work front.

The very next day I got a phone call saying, "Hi Reg, you've got an interview on Monday morning in the Nero's coffee house at 10 o'clock. I'll see you there, what do you know about electrical work?"

"Naff all," I replied.

"Oh well," sighed Paul, "I still think you're the man for the job. I'll see you tomorrow."

So the next day I went to the coffee house for a very exclusive interview with Mr Paul Tooley.

His words were, "I'll cut to the chase, you've got the job if you want it and you'll be working with a giant Russian fella called Igor. I'll match your joinery shop rate, but the only thing is, you'll be working nights and it's a seven-week contract. What do you think Reg?"

"But what have I got to do Paul?"

"Whatever the big Russian lad says. Also you're a first-aider aren't you?"

"Well I've been on most of the courses through my skiing escapades but that's about it."

"Well," said Paul, "that's perfect 'cos you'll be working in shops and it's law that when anyone is working with electricity late at night in shops the electrician must have a buddy. Just in case. You see, your mate could be dealing with anything up to 500 volts, so I want you to look after him and that's your job."

"Well," I said, "I'll take the job on the understanding that if I'm not living up to your expectations you get rid of me straight away, as in this case mates don't come into the equation."

"It's a deal," said Paul.

As we were shaking hands the sun seemed to disappear as if there was a total eclipse, and in walked the giant of a man, Mr Igor. I said to Paul quietly. "You want me to look after him? It should be the other way round." Paul introduced us and we got on like a house on fire, and within half an hour I was a qualified sparky's mate.

When Igor left, Paul and I went back to Paul's office where he had most of the dates of the forthcoming soul events. Paul started to work out my rota so that I didn't miss any of them. I thought to myself, yet another Soulie putting himself out to help someone with his back against the wall. These marvellous people never cease to amaze me.

After completing the seven-week contract, I had enough woodwork booked in to set me up for the rest of the year so everything was good. On Thursday the 13th April, Jon Buck promoted one of his RSG (Ready Steady Go) soul club reunions. He managed to hire the Unicorn nightclub in Leighton Buzzard. It's the same venue where Jon used to run the RSG's all those years ago, and what a night this turned out to be. There were so many old faces there, people we hadn't seen for years turned out for this special night. Everything about the night was brilliant, until about midnight when all the lights went out and the record being played came to a slurry stop.

We only had a bloody power cut didn't we! But this didn't dampen the spirits of the night; it was as if it was meant to be. Because we couldn't play any more sounds, it gave us all a chance to chat and catch up with each other. Also, I was on a nervous high that night as the next day I was on my way to the Austrian Alps to take the ski exam to become an Alpine Ski Leader.

Just before I left the Unicorn, Jenny Knight strolled over to me and said, "Good Luck Reg, when will you know if you've passed or not?"

"Well Jen" I replied, "Apparently my coach reckons if I come home in one piece I've passed."

"Stop it," says Jen. "You'd better come home. Who will I have to take the piss out of if you don't? Anyway I want you to bring me back some of that alpine chocolate."

"Okay Jen, give us a big kiss in case I don't come back and I'll see you in ten days' time."

The next day, after loading all my ski equipment on the coach, I looked up at the window and there was one of my skiing companions, Tricia Mackenzie, who happened to be taking the same exam. So, we teamed up for the week as buddies and managed to pass the Alpine Ski Leader exam at a fairly decent level, you might say in old school terms with credit.

When Peter Gillespie-Silver the ski coach announced how well Trish and I had done, I looked up to heaven with tears streaming down my face and said, "Mum, I know this is the year you died and this is hard for me to say but life couldn't be richer. I won't speak too soon though, but I do believe I'm about to turn the corner and look life straight in the eye again."

A few weeks later my wife Debbie received her compensation (after damaging her back through slipping on some posters that were lying on the floor in Tesco's). Debbie only got half of the money that she owed, but through wheeling and dealing, we managed to pay off all the creditors and although we haven't got anything to show for Debbie's accident, at least we don't owe anything to anyone. So I've decided to try and buy my house again instead of just paying the interest. I know it's a little bit late in life but I'm beginning to see the light at the end of the tunnel and full dignity has been restored.

So with life looking a lot sweeter, it was back to some full time souling. Karen Bedford phoned me up and said, "Right Reg I've managed to book up the Caister Soul Weekender, it's the 28th April till the 1st May. The only problem is the site is fully booked so we might have to stay in a bed and breakfast. What do you think? Also I need to know if Debbie is okay about the two of us going off for the weekend."

"Well," I replied, "Debbie won't mind but I would be a lot happier if I can use my Mum's caravan. It's situated on a small campsite about three miles away from where the weekender is being held. Give me ten minutes and I'll phone you back, I'll speak to Debbie and ask my Dad if the caravan is free that weekend."

Within a few minutes I phoned Karen back and everything is sorted.

In no time at all the 28th April had arrived. So off we set. As on this occasion it was just the two of us in my car, we could take whatever we wanted. With the back seat down in my Vauxhall Estate, there was plenty of room to take my little record player, a rake of sounds and the best part of Karen's wardrobe. Why do women take away a year's worth of clothes, shoes and make-up for a four day break? They never cease to amaze me.

We arrived at the Vauxhall Holiday Park where the Caister Soul Weekenders are held nowadays, and after queuing for our weekend passes, we went straight into the main ballroom. We met Suzanne, Janet, Nettie, Sharon, Steve, Hutch and some of our friends who DJ at Caister such as Harvey, Pete Collins, Maggot (Tony Matthews) Frostie and the drop-dead gorgeous Ronnie O'Brian, a friend of mine who also plays on Sunday nights for the Solar radio station. Her show is called *Insatiable Soul*, so all in all, Karen and I were in the presence of the most exceptional company.

The first thing our Sharon says to me was, "I wish I knew it was just the two of you in your car, I could have loaded it up with some of my clothes and shoes, you should have told me." Whilst looking at Sharon, shaking my head, I said, "You're all the bloody same, you birds. I can't understand it, you all take away enough clothes at the weekend to sink a bloody battleship and when you all get all dolled up for the evening, you come out wearing next to nothing. I'm not even going to contemplate trying to understand the female mind, I wouldn't ever dream of going down that road."

As usual the first night of the weekender (Friday) was a blinder. The very best dancers were all out on the floor. In my opinion the Friday and

Saturday nights are when the hardcore dancers are at their best, mainly because if you're dancing from 12 noon to 4 in the morning, four days on the trot, by the Sunday the old legs start complaining that they have been overworked. That's when the old soft-shoe shuffle comes into its own and everyone starts bopping on the spot. The Caister dancers won't stop dancing at any cost, they still have exceptional rhythm even when tiredness creeps in and they go into their soft-shoe-shuffling mode.

It was on the Friday night when I pointed out to Karen one of my favourite jazz/funk dancers. I only know him by the name of Glen; some of the Soulies call him Catweasle. He is a thin chap with long hair in a ponytail with a little goatee beard, just like Catweasle. His appearance is nothing like a soul fan, but he is the best dancer I've ever seen. I know I raved about Tom when I was younger and I find it difficult to separate the skills of both dancers. It's like comparing George Best to Stanley Matthews; there are so many years between their movements in time. I find I have to go back to the old cliché, Tom was the best in the late seventies and in the year of 2006, Glen is the man! I don't know if Glen graduated from the Rave or the Latin Jazz scene, but when he's on that floor, in my opinion, he rules the roost—his dance moves are exceptional. One minute he's dancing like the Latin Jazz dancers then all of a sudden he will place his hand on top of his head and appear to be pushing his body into the ground. A few seconds later, his legs fold up and he ends up like a splodge on the floor, then through his body movements he appears to start growing like a plant out of the ground—it's brilliant to watch. Bloody hard to describe but looks fantastic; Glen is, by far, my dancer of the moment.

During the Friday night when Karen had disappeared, gallivanting with some of her mates, I found myself in the Latin Jazz clubroom where Ronnie O'Brian was dancing. I always try to have a dance with Ronnie as she is trying to teach me the Latin Jazz dance moves. I do feel that I'm getting there slowly, but I'm fifty-two for Christ's sake and I'm beginning to feel my age, what with the Northern, Latin Jazz, Soul dancing and the Soft Shoe shuffle it's bound to take its toll. But as I have said before, the only way I will stop dancing is when the big man upstairs gives me a call.

Whilst I was in the clubroom, I heard that my old mate Maggot (Tony Matthews) was playing the sounds of Philadelphia in T-Zone so off I trot. T-Zone is the smallest room at Caister but when filled with the right people, the atmosphere is electric. When the likes of Maggot are playing their idea of Soul music, it's a job to get into the place. As soon as I arrived at T-Zone, I squeezed my way through the crowd to the back of the room and being so small I could get away with standing on a chair. As soon as Maggot saw me, he started shuffling his fingers through his record box, then when the sound he was playing had finished, he announced the next with, "My next record is especially for Reg, he knows why." As soon as the next record had kicked in, my friend Janet of the St. Albans' crew rushes over, grabs my hand and says, "It couldn't be better Reg" because the record that Maggot was playing for me was 'I'll Always Love My Mama' by The Intruders.

Whilst standing on the chair, I caught Maggot's eye with a big smile and a wave of acknowledgement. Every record Maggot played in this last hour was exceptional, and as always when you're enjoying yourself the time flies. In no time at all it was four o'clock in the morning. I found Karen in the main arena sitting by the stage complaining about her feet.

I asked, "Why are your feet hurting then sister? It's only the first night and I'm ten years older than you. Are you wearing the appropriate shoes? Let me help you up. Are you hungry? Only I'm going to get a seafood cocktail off the old geezers stall by the main entrance door."

Karen replied, "You go and get your prawn cocktail then we'll go back to your Mum's caravan. I've had it, I'm absolutely shattered."

On the way back to the caravan I take a different route, then Karen asked, "Where are you going?"

I replied, "I just want to see what time this scrap yard opens."

"Why have you got something to scrap then?"

"Yes," I said. "You."

"Why me?" says Karen.

"Well you're no good to me if you only last one night, this is a Soul Weekender, a four night special, I can see I'm gonna need a younger model. Next time I'm thinking of bringing young Emma Weedall, she's only twenty-three. I bet Emma would last the full weekend."

Well the look on Karen's face when she replied was a picture, "Bloody cheek, there's no way I'm ready for the scrap yard. I'll out dance you tomorrow. Scrap yard, you're havin' a laugh Reg."

Although on these Caister Soul Weekenders, I don't get to sleep until four thirty am, I'm always awake at around about nine thirty the next morning. I start the day by making Karen and myself a cup of tea. At about ten o'clock I normally go for a swim for about an hour, it's good to have a swim in between the dance times, as it seems to revitalise your legs ready for the next fourteen hours on the dance floor. At about eleven thirty, I wake up whoever I'm Souling with, in this case it's Karen 'My feet are killing me' Bedford. Then I make something to eat, my speciality is the little Reg jacket potato filled with cheese, a glass of milk or a cup of tea and a piece of fruit; apple, orange, banana or whatever takes your fancy. After we've eaten we get ready for the afternoon session.

Karen and I left Mum's caravan at about twelve thirty, as I wanted to be in the main arena by one o'clock, mainly because my old mate Pete Collins was the first DJ of the day playing his 'choons' from one o'clock till two. After Pete's set, Karen and I head for the BBQ area where the selected DJs play the Caister anthems from days gone by, which gets everybody in the party mood. Around about six o'clock the DJs stop playing for a couple of hours so everybody can get ready for the highlight of the weekend, the Saturday night fancy dress night.

The management of the Soul Weekenders set the theme for the fancy dress nights. On this particular occasion, the theme was the Mardi Gras Carnival but I do believe the organisers are running out of ideas, because on the Caister website they are asking the Soulies to come up with their own ideas. So far on these Saturday nights, with my friend Suzanne I've been a Mod, Mini Me and an Evacuee! At the Mardi Gras, I wore a flowery shirt with a flower garland around my neck, a bit boring really but I still felt the part. The rest of the weekend is pretty much the same, making sure you're in the right place at the right time so as not to miss your favourite DJs, dancing till you drop and finishing the evening with a seafood cocktail at four o'clock in the morning then trying to get some sleep as soon as your head hits the pillow, so you're bright and fresh after your swim ready to do it all over again.

Karen and I are trying to encourage some more of the Northern Soul fans to attend the Caister Soul Weekenders to broaden their views of Soul music. It's good to hear the sounds right across the board so when you're in conversation you can comment on the 'choons' you like and the ones you don't. I believe the only way you can say if you don't like something, is to put yourself right in the middle of what it is you think you don't like, before you can comment on its quality or not. My visits to the Caister Soul Weekenders are getting better and better. I don't really know why, maybe it's because I'm learning a lot more about Soul music from the different sources of followers or it might be because I'm recognising the 'choons' from the previous visits. The one thing I have noticed is the companionship and friendliness is overwhelming whether you're into Northern, Jazz, Funk or Soul.

Whilst travelling back to Hemel Hempstead from Caister, the thoughts running through my mind were: "Is it just my turn to have a really good year or is it just panning out this way due to friends making things happen for me? I'm having a really good year and it's only early May. Perhaps this is the year I should try and do something with my book."

Just then my thoughts were disturbed when Karen asked, "Are you all right, Reg you're awfully quiet."

I replied, "I'm not too bad, just a bit tired, I was just thinking about my book."

Karen then says, "I think you should try and do something with it, why don't you run it past Annie Chase, she's a school teacher and Annie's certainly been on the scene a long time."

"I might just do that when I see her next, I've had a brilliant weekend Karen, I'll give Susie and Shaz a ring when I get back to make sure they got home all right."

"Will that be before you've played the new records you've bought or after?"

"What do you think Karen?" (After).

Some of my favourite 'choons' from those Caister Soul Weekenders are:

Every Day	Sunburst Band
Bring The Family Back	Billy Paul
My Life	Chanelle
Just Be Thankfull	Omar & Angie Stone
Sex Machine (Remix)	James Brown
Let's Get It On (Remix)	Marvin Gaye
Love To The Music	Temptations
I'll Always Love My Mama	The Intruders
Who's Gonner Love You When I've Gone	The Imperials
Take It To The Bank	Bill Summers
Overdose Of Joy	Eugene Record
Sugar Pie Guy	The Joneses
Ain't No Stopping Us Now	Mcfadden & Whitehead
Brazilian Love Affair	George Duke
Does She Have A Friend For Me	Gene Chandler

Oh dear, I could go on writing this list forever; there are so many brilliant 'choons' out there. I find my favourites are changing every week. Also, trying to keep up with all aspects of Soul music works out quite expensive, but I do what I can to improve my record collection. As I am out of the woods, money-wise, I am trying to replace some of my English pressings with the original copies without the wife knowing.

Her normal quote is, "You've already got this record haven't you?"

Then I reply, "Course I have, but Chris asked me if I could get him a copy!" as I place the pressing in my sales box at nowhere near the price of the original.

Shortly after returning from Caister, Yogi phoned me up to say, "We're off to Hitchin Soul Club this Friday". So as you can see, there's never a dull moment, as soon as we return from one event were off to another, just like when we were kids. Whilst I was checking that I had everything in my Soul bag, I had an inkling that Annie Chase might be attending the Soul night so I threw a couple of chapters of my book in my bag.

On entering the Hitchin Soul Club I noticed that some of the normal faces were already there; Chris, Lorraine, Jenny, Special Kay, her husband Ian, Winston. In the middle of the floor was Annie. another of my favourite dancers; once again there is a touch of uniqueness in Annie's moves and her timing, she appears to know every beat of every record kicking out her foot or raising her arm at the right moment, and when Annie raises her arms together, her appearance is like a puppet being controlled by strings. I like Annie's dancing so much I am always trying to imitate her dance moves. I believe this is the way to becoming a good dancer yourself. If you like certain moves by other dancers, try to add them to your own. After all, dancing is just body movement to music. Once you get the timing and the rhythm right you start to become a good dancer yourself.

Once Yogi and I had settled where we were going to leave our soul bags, we headed over towards the bar area where I got us both a drink. Whilst supping my pint of lager top I noticed that Annie had left the dance floor and was sitting by the entrance door, so I left Yogi chatting to Pete Tebbutt and made my way over to where Annie is sitting.

"All right Annie? I've brought a couple of chapters from my book to run past you when you've got a minute."

To my amazement Annie replied, "Brilliant Reg let's go in the other bar where it's a lot quieter, I've been told by some of the other Soulies about what you're trying to do. It doesn't matter if you struggle to read and write, there are always ways around these problems. When I've read what you're trying to say, I will imagine that I have no idea who you are."

When Annie and I entered the bar she found a table while I got a drink each. Whilst waiting to be served I looked over at Annie who wasn't just flicking through the pages, she was reading the pieces of paper, word for word. Once I got our drinks, I sat beside her after about thirty long seconds.

Annie took a sip of her drink and said, "I love it Reg. I bloody love it. What I like about what you've written is, as I am reading the story, I start wondering about different things I would have liked you to mention. Then when I turn the page those things are there in black and white; the microphones hanging over the balcony, the smell, the heat and just reading the first five pages of this particular chapter, I have tingles running up and down my arms. You must see if you can do something more with these memories; perhaps Mike Ritson might be interested? You never know."

Well, I thought to myself, Annie couldn't have said anything nicer and through her comments, Annie has certainly given me the will to carry on and finish writing down my idea of Soul music. Three quarters of an hour later we both stroll back to the Soul night and all our mates asked, "Where have you two been?"

Annie said, "I've been outside with Reg and it was wonderful!" leaving just a few thoughts to the Soulies' imaginations.

On the Saturday of June 3rd I felt that I had reached the pinnacle of my DJing escapades when Taffy Guy asked if I could play an hour's spot at the Southgate all-dayer, playing alongside some of the best DJs in the business. The Southgate all-dayer is a Soul do that used to be run by Randy Couzens and some of his mates. But nowadays as Randy Couzens is no longer with us, his son Terry and Taffy Guy are adamant that this must carry on in memory of the man that everybody loved; the man who described the Soul scene as 'this thing of ours'. To my mind, this is a wonderful statement. So, being asked to play my idea of Soul music at this special event was a great honour.

On the day, I travelled down to Southgate with Jon and Sue Buck, we arrived around mid-day and already the Sun public house where the all-dayers are held was starting to fill up. My plan was to play my 'choons', meet Karen Bedford at the all-dayer, stay till about seven o'clock, then head off to the Night Shift Club at the Bisley Pavilion. I was going to meet Alan Eames, as he was trying to get some records on the original labels for me, so a full day's Souling was in store. Once I got settled, and sorted out where we were going to sit, Jon passed me a drink, then my mate Toby strolled over, sat next to me and we started shuffling through our record boxes, both admiring each other's rarities and collectable items. Toby's records were a lot rarer than mine but I'm working on it and if Alan Eames can get me the records I'm asking for, it will be a good start.

After about an hour, young Terry strolled over and said, "Okay Reg, it's your turn on the decks."

I gathered my records together and headed towards the disco stand. Just before I was about to set my first record up, Jon plugged in an old telephone hand piece to the queuing up terminal, which made setting up the records a lot easier. I started my set off with 'These Memories' by Almetta Lattimore, then as it was only two o'clock in the afternoon, I proceeded with some mid tempo classics such as:

No One There	Martha Reeves
Making My Daydream Real	We The People
Overdose Of Joy	Eugene Record
Colour Him Father	O.C. Smith
Let Her Go	Otis Smith

Then I thought I'd try my 'choon' of the moment, which was called 'Treasure The Moment' by The Pioneers. After about thirty seconds of playing time both Taffy and Toby looked up and said, "What's this Reg?"

"It's the record I told you about Taff; the one Marcus from Treacle Soul gave me. It's by The Pioneers."

I passed Taff the LP cover and as soon as he saw the front of it he turned to me and said, "I can't believe it. I've seen this LP loads of times, but I've only ever looked at the picture of the gorgeous bird on the cover and not at the contents of the music."

"Shame on you Taffy and I thought you were a connoisseur of the music."

Taffy replied, "There's not many that slips my net Reg, but this one did; it's a lovely record."

Yes, I thought. I've finally got a 'choon' that Taffy likes and he hasn't got—but this is only one of mine to his hundreds that I would like. After playing my set a few people clapped and I thought I'd done all right, because when you are playing early you don't look for a packed floor of dancers, you look for smiles and foot tappers. I asked the chap waiting to take over from me what his name was. "Mike, Mike Ritson."

So when my last record finished, I said to the crowd, "Thanks for listening and I'll hand you over to Mike," and to my amazement his first record was also 'These Memories' by Almeta Lattimore. What a lovely record it is, I personally wouldn't mind if every DJ started their set with that 'choon' as it's that good.

It was only when I stepped down from the podium and made my way to the bar that I felt quite pleased with my efforts, especially when the likes of Terry (Randy's son), Taff and Toby commented on what a lovely set I played. Yes, you could say I was well pleased.

It was around about four o'clock when my plans for the day were about to change. Jon Buck asked if I could travel back to Hemel with him and Sue. Jon's wife Sue had been ill for quite a long time now, Sue suffers from Multiple Sclerosis (MS) and Jon's job is to make Sue as comfortable as he possibly can. So in the little bit of spare time that he has, Jon has managed to build Sue a mobile home from a box-type van with all the necessary facilities such as a wheelchair lift, shower, storage place for her small scooter and a luxurious bedroom. Jon and Sue have been everywhere in their mobile home and he was about to embark on another adventure by taking Sue to the Bisley Nightshift club and staying the night in the mobile home before moving on to the New Forest.

The reason Jon wanted me to travel back to Hemel was to get the van ready for their week away. I tried to phone Karen to tell her that I wouldn't be at Southgate when she arrived, but I couldn't get in contact with her. Then I thanked Terry and Taff for letting me DJ and asked Taff to look out for Karen, as I had to leave. Then Jon, Sue and I left the Southgate all-dayer. When we were just about to leave the M25 at the Hemel turnoff John suddenly cried, "Oh no, I've only left my bloody telephone handset on the DJ stand."

"I'm sure someone will look after it till you come back from your holiday Jon."

"But I need it for tonight, I'm DJing at Bisley."

Just as Jon was drifting into a state of despair, my mobile phone rings and it's Karen asking where I am, so I explained to Karen that I am helping Jon and Sue get their mobile home ready as Jon is taking Sue away for the week.

Then Karen said, "If that's the case I'll let you off Reg, are you still going to Bisley?"

"Of course I am," I replied, "but as I'm in Hemel I'll get Yogi to take me."

"Will he take me as well if I can get to Hemel?"

"Yeah of course he will, but you'll have to be here by eight o'clock."

"That's great Reg. I'll see you later then."

"Oh and Karen, we need you to do us a favour. Can you go to the DJ stand and ask the DJ for Jon's telephone handset as he needs it to cue in his records at Bisley."

"Okay Reg, it's sorted, I'll see you guys later."

Once Jon and I had got working on his van we were all done and dusted within the hour, the time then was about five forty-five, which gave me time to shower, chill out and reflect back on what a smashing day I was having. And it was only half time! Roll on eight o'clock. As I had some time to kill whilst waiting for Karen and Yogi, I sorted out and put my records back in my main record box. Debbie asked how I got on playing my 'choons' amongst some of the best DJs in the country.

I replied, "It was a great experience. The Southgate all-dayer is a smashing day out and when I had found out that I had a record that impressed Toby & Taff, well it was just the icing on the cake."

Not before long, there was a double toot of a car horn outside my house, Yogi and Karen had arrived and we were on our way to Bisley. As soon as I got into Yogi's car, Karen passed me the telephone handset. I immediately sent Jon a text saying we're on our way with his record cueing device.

When we arrived at Bisley, Jon and Alan Eames greeted us at the entrance door. I passed Jon the telephone handset, he then turned round to Karen and said, "Thank you, Kaz, I would have been lost without it."

"You should have seen the trouble I had to go through to get it. But that's another story." I thought Karen was trying to wind Jon up. I had no idea what she was going on about.

Alan then turned to me and said, "I've got one of the records you asked for Reg."

"Which one?" I asked.

"The demo of 'I'll See You When I Git There' by Lou Rawls. I've got another Philly sound you're gonna love called 'A Nice Girl Like You' by The Intruders."

"Brilliant," I replied, "I'll have them both." What a day this is turning out to be. "Al, is there any chance I can hear the Intruders' sound?"

"Of course you can," replied Alan from under the table where his records were set out. He pulls out a small battery record player, places a copy of 'A Nice Girl Like You' on the deck and just before the 'choon' kicks in, I call Karen over. "See what you think of this 'choon' that Alan's got for me Kaz. I want your expert opinion."

Karen replied, "Yeah I'm sure you do." She strolled over and puts her arm around my shoulder and Alan says, "Not another girlfriend Reg, how many have you got?"

"Hundreds mate. There's no problems having hundreds of girlfriends mate but it don't 'arf get bloody dear at Christmas. And if the truth was known, I really love them all."

Then Alan looks at Yogi and says, "What we gonna do with him Yogi?"

"It's all right for you and Karen, I've had to put up with him all me life!"

Then I piped up with, "Stop picking on me and put my record on."

When the record reaches the chorus the lyrics are, *'How does a nice girl like you fall in love with a bad guy like me'*. At this point Karen laughs and says, "Well that just about sums it up, don't it!"

"What do I owe you then Al?"

"Twenty pounds Reg."

"What did you say? Fifteen?"

"Alright Reg, fifteen and your girlfriend." Well I looked at the record, then I looked at Karen, then I looked at the record, then I looked at Karen and said, "Sorry mate you've gotta go."

"Bloody cheek, you're swapping me for a piece of vinyl."

I placed my records in my bag and said, "You're too late sister, the deal is struck!" As I started to walk away smiling, Karen, with a frown, says to Alan, "Don't you just love him? He's got more front than Sainsburys."

About twenty minutes later we're all on the dance floor and the fun we were having by Alan's record stall carries on when I say to Karen, "Don't dance too close to me, you belong to Alan now."

"Yeah right Reg, where you gonna find another mate as nice as me?"

At that moment the timing couldn't have been better, when a good looking French girl taps me on the shoulder and asks if I could show her some of the dance steps.

"What," I said, "you want me to show you? There are a lot better dancers than me out there."

Then the true sense of her humour came into its own as the French girl was a girl after my own heart. She replied in a French accent, "Yes I know, but I don't want to set my sights too high do I?"

"Very funny," I replied, "what's your name?"

"My name is Marion."

"Where do you live in France?"

"I live in Champagne."

"So you live in Champagne and I suppose you want to dance as good as champagne tastes."

"Yes please," Marion replied, so I grab her hand and take her over to where Karen and Yogi were standing and said, "I want you to meet my new girlfriend from Champagne in France. Her name is Marion."

Whilst Yogi was shaking her hand, I believed he whispered something to her in French, being a clever old sod, and then the wind-up was on me. Every time a record stopped I would say to him, "What did you say?"

After about five records and fifteen minutes later Yogi said, "I said to Marion 'You must have shit in your eyes and be deaf listening to anything Reg has to say'." We laughed our bloody heads off. It seems that every time we go out of our houses it's non stop laughter all the time, especially sharing company with people who have a sense of humour to die for and are up for it all the time. We could have all rounded this superb day off by going back to Jon and Sue's mobile home for a cup of coffee, but as the time was two o'clock in the morning Yogi, Karen and I decided to call it a day and what a brilliant day. Saturday June 3rd 2006 especially as another two sounds had reached my record box.

The next day, I went onto my computer, logged into *Soul Source* and read all the feedback of the Southgate all-dayer. Then I browsed through all the brilliant photos that Darcie had loaded on the *Soul Source* members' gallery. There was a really nice photo of Martin Ainsworth, Toby and me. The photo would have been a lot better if Toby had opened his eyes, but it was midday and he had drunk a couple of 'Shandies'—need I say more?

Some of the big differences between Souling nowadays and what it was like in the past, is that we don't have to travel so far to hear the top 'choons' and we are spoilt for choice, whereas all those years ago, you could count the main venues on one hand and most of them were over two hundred miles away from where I lived. In the past, it was like selected people from all over the UK were called to participate in a ritual held in these wonderful places; you could say it was like an obsession.

Then there were the clothes we all wore, although we all loved our fashions of the time, nowadays we are still fashion conscious, but we don't follow suit so much. Whether you're the type who likes to dress like we did in the past or someone who likes to dress in the latest styles, it doesn't matter. Chris and Yogi like to wear the baggy Wigan breeches with bowling shirts, Karen on the other hand likes to wear a smart modern trouser and on top just a sports type bra and a cardigan. Kay looks her best wearing a mini skirt and her knee-length boots and as for me, I like to dress younger than I am. My son Jack is quite a smart dude himself and I have often been known to take a browse through his wardrobe and nick one of his smart shirts to wear for my evening out. I do own a pair of Prince of Wales checked strides, half a dozen Fred Perrys and a Barathear blazer. But as far as button down Ben Shermans are concerned, they do nothing for me nowadays as this kind of shirt is tailored to fit by a pleat down the back and taken in darts just above the waist. They look dead sharp on Lads and Lassies with normal shape bodies, but if you've got a bit of a belly like me, get yourself a nice baggy bowling shirt and wear it on the outside—it's inclined to make you look a bit slimmer than you really are!

The one thing that hasn't changed much are the shoes. An all leather shoe is a must if you're thinking of dancing for fourteen hours or more. I personally prefer a lace up Brogue or flat top, loafers are okay but they're a slip-on shoe and if you're doing some extreme dancing they're likely to slip off! If you're a hardcore dancer, wear what you feel most comfortable in and don't take any notice of what anyone else thinks. If someone is knocking your style of dress, it's because either they have too much time on their hands, they can't dance as well as you or are just jealous. Also, there's the age range of dancers nowadays. As we are getting older, most of us have children who have probably been brainwashed by us parents playing our music all the time. In my case, my kids hate my 'choons', but if in your case your kids like the music, take them with you. At Caister nowadays the weekends are becoming more of a family affair and some of the kids really know how to get down in the groove when they are on the dance floor.

Please don't complain about youngsters being out with adults; they need to be there, these kids are going to carry on the Soul scene when all us Soulies are long gone. My favourite young dancer at this present time isn't a Jazz Funk dancer, Street or Latin. This young person is a Northern Soul dancer and in my opinion one of the best, her name is Natalie Smith, aged thirteen. Natalie is the daughter of one of my mates, Sue, who is quite a sharp dancer herself. When Natalie is dancing, it is inevitable that you are going to see some of her mother's moves in her dance steps. I believe when she starts to feel the music from within, individual movements will start entering the equation and in no time at all Natalie will truly be one of the great dancers of her time. When she's out there on the floor. Natalie already has a good ear for the music, as one of her favourites is 'Independent Woman' by Jan Jones. What a brilliant record it is. It's one of my favourites too, so well done Natalie. I hope you get the same buzz as I've had being a Soul fan because once it grabs you, I'm afraid it's for life.

On the tenth of June 2006, things started to move on the LD scooter that I'm rebuilding. My mate from the past, Tony Lock wanted to spray the frame, side panels and leg shields, but as he was so busy, he could only manage to do the side panels. So another friend Mark Thompson came to the rescue and within a couple of days the scooter frame was all sprayed up to the highest standard and was looking good, or so we thought, but our nightmare was just about to begin.

As the scooter started out its life in 1957, by the time I acquired it forty-eight years later it was as rotten as a pear. Most of my mates told me to throw it in a skip because it was that bad. The leg shield floor was like a sieve and beyond repair. Through another friend (Suedie) Paul Bryant, I managed to get another set of leg shields; this set had a half decent floor with a naff front, our idea was to cut them in half and weld the two good bits together. I had this done by a local metal fabricator. It was when Mark and I offered them to the already painted frame we noticed that the leg shields were about an inch too long 'what a bloody nightmare'. But Mark being a positive kind of chap said, "Right Reg, lift them off and we'll cut them in half again." Once the leg shields were in two pieces we bolted the floor and the front piece into their respective positions, marked where the two pieces overlapped and cut the excess inch off. Then with tremendous skill Mark welded them back together in situ. As the metal was like tissue paper, we did have to case the weld a bit, but by the time Mark had finished the job was perfect.

The main reason we kept working on this particular scooter against all odds was because of its sentimental value, you see Peter Mulinger rebuilt the scooter engine. The seats were paid for by my Mum and through the log book I found out that the first ever owner of the scooter was still alive and lived in Leverstock Green, just two miles away from where I lived. So you might say we were on a mission to complete the project. Because Peter Mulinger was so enthusiastic about the scooter world, he told me he couldn't wait to start the work on my engine. He too had an LD, which he wanted to restore, so his idea was to practice on mine before he started work on his own but sadly three weeks after completing the job on my engine, Peter was taken away from us. His family and the scooter world will sadly miss him. And then there was my Mum, because she was my Mum.

Once Mark had sprayed the leg shields, they, along with the side panels, were all sent to Simon Clark, a top class air brusher, for the final touches. He took ages, but as you all know you can't rush an artist. So, whilst waiting for the artwork, I fitted the engine to the frame and managed to get everything working. I even had a ride around the small industrial estate where I live so I could do some final adjustments on the cables that you pre-fit before the bodywork. All through the summer months, at the weekends I would tinker about with the scooter.

On Saturdays though, I would always be tidied up and finished by four o'clock in the afternoon, mainly so I could chill out for a few hours before Yogi picked me up to go Souling.

We were Souling nearly every weekend; it was one of those red hot summers where everybody had a feel-good factor about themselves, and as the circumstances have changed money-wise, we always came back with records—loads of them. It appeared to me that we were both upgrading our collections by adding to them. Also we were buying some of the 'choons' we already had, if we came across an original in a better condition. We were living life to the full and loving every minute of it and before I knew it, it was mid-September.

But I still had received no scooter panels. In a conversation I was having one night with Karen her answer to the situation was, "I know you want to get your scooter finished by Christmas, Reg. But as you said before, you can't hurry an artist. Why don't you leave it for a couple of weeks then ring Simon when we get back."

"Get back from where," I asked?

"Caister of course, I've booked up for the Autumn Weekender, it's September 29th, 30th and the 1st of October. I booked it early so we could all get on the site where it's being held. Then hopefully when we get back all your scooter bits will be painted up ready for you to fit."

"Hang on a minute Kaz. I can't get a word in edgeways. Yes, I'm up for it but who's all?"

"Well it's me, you, Emma Hagans, her friend Graham Hill, then I was thinking of advertising for two more on *Soul Source* as we've been allocated a six berth caravan. All the four berth ones had gone."

"We could have got six in Mum's caravan."

"I know but little Emma's adamant she wants to be on site."

"Okay so when are we all going then?"

"Between three and four weeks time."

"Wow, that soon, I don't know where this year has gone, it's flown past. I'm looking forward to introducing Emma to some of my mates.

It will be like Northern Soul meets Jazz Funk; I hope Emma likes the music."

A couple of days later Karen phones me up and says, "You'll never guess, someone has only answered the advert and wants to come to Caister with us and her name is Lorna Fry, do you know a Lorna Fry, Reg?"

"No, not that I can think of, but it looks like we soon will."

On the Friday of the twenty-ninth of September I arrived at Karen's house in Potter's Bar around about 1pm. Whilst I was loading Karen's 'twenty seven holdalls plus vat' in the back of my car, a posh car pulls up along side, driving the car was a really stunning looking blonde with piercing blue eyes.

I was just about to say 'sorry, I can't give you any directions I'm new to the area' when this women says, "Hi are you Reg? My name is Lorna, I'm coming to Caister with you."

All of a sudden I felt just like Hugh Heffner. I told Lorna to put her car on Karen's driveway. As Lorna pulled off the road I noticed a large Liverpool football club sticker on the back window of her posh car.

When she got out of the car I said, "You don't support that shower of shit do you."

Lorna's reply was, "Oh no, there's not a problem already is there?"

"Of course there isn't sister," as I raised my shirt sleeve to show her the Liverpool tattoo on my right arm, "I support them as well but I'm afraid I'm beyond repair. I've supported them all of me life." I then loaded Lorna's bags into the car and off we set.

Travelling to Caister, Karen was in charge of the music. I've only got a cassette player but it was good enough in this case. Lorna and I were talking about Liverpool Football Club. We had one stop on the way for something to eat then in no time at all we were at the Vauxhall holiday park. If you can prove to the security chap on the main gate that you're a "Caister Elite", in other words that you have been to at least ten weekenders, you're allowed some small privileges. Like instead of having to park your car in the car park, you can take the car straight to the door of your caravan. In my case, when I am a Caister elite, taking my car to where my caravan is situated is going to be a major plus. I won't have to start the weekend with elongated arms due to carrying all those bloody clothes the girls take with them (which they hardly ever wear).

On this occasion when I pulled up at the entrance instead of heading towards the car park I pulled up right outside the main gate, the guy looked at me through the windscreen, lifted up the barrier and waved me through. Karen said, "How the hell did you manage that?"

"I don't know, I just went with the flow. He was looking at me through the windscreen for some reason."

Then at that moment we realised what had happened. On my windscreen there's a mock disabled sticker with the symbol of a person in a wheelchair with a crossed plaster on the side of his head with the words "Disabled, Deafened by the Funk". We think the guy on the gate might have let us in for that reason but the fact of the matter was that we managed to get the car on site and that was good enough for us. We then thought it would be better to park the car next to the caravan before we collected our weekend passes as Emma and Graham had already arrived.

Karen rang Emma on her mobile to ask where we are staying and all I heard was Karen saying, "You're joking what a result! We'll be there in a couple of seconds."

Then Karen turned to me and said "Not only have we got the car on site, we're in one of those posh chalets as well."

I replied, "Really I feel like a Caister elitist already and I've still got another two weekenders to attend before I actually become one."

Once we were all settled in our posh chalet, after about half an hour the thoughts going through my mind were 'wow what a brilliant little crew we have this time'. I had only known Lorna and Emma's friend Graham for a matter of hours. We felt like we had known each other for most of our lives. Although we were all at Caister for the music and the dancing, some of the best times we had were in our chalet. The friendships that had grown between us all were second to none and what I mostly liked when we were altogether in the chalet was playing our music. I didn't only take my small record player this time, I also took a CD player as well just in case some of the others purchased some CDs from Gary Dennis's record store and wanted to play them.

On the Friday night, none of us got in until about 4.30 in the morning. The night was exactly like all the other times before—absolutely brilliant. As I've said before, it doesn't seem to make any difference the time I get in, I am always up around about ten o'clock, so not wanting to disturb the others I go for a swim. I normally take about an hour and a half. At about quarter to twelve I got back to the chalet. Emma was prancing about in the kitchen and the others were still in bed. I made myself a couple of slices of toast and a cup of tea then Emma and I sat down and had breakfast together. Although we all think we know each other when were out Souling, it's not until you actually live with your friends for a couple of days you start to realise what great company these people really are. Whilst Emma and I were having breakfast, Emma asked what records I'd brought with me.

"Just a selection of Soul and Jazz Funk really, I didn't fetch any Northern. It's not the weekend for Northern."

Emma then said, "Do you think I will like any of records you've brought with you Reg?"

"Oh yes you will Emm, this weekend is not all about that hand clapping, back dropping, spinny, bouncy stuff."

As the others were starting to stir I asked, "Do any of you mind if I play any of my music guys?"

"Only if you play a couple of tracks off my new CD," Lorna cries, "It's on the table"

Emma passed me the CD. I put my glasses on to scan the tracks and I noticed the live version of 'Distant Lovers' by Marvin Gaye, so I set both the record player and the CD player up ready for my early morning Soul session.

I started with one for the ladies 'There's No Me Without You' by Chairman Of The Board, then I continued with:

'Could Heaven Ever Be Like This'	Idris Mohammed
'Call Me'	Al Green
'Let's Get It On'	Marvin Gaye Remix
'My Life'	Chanelle
'Daylight'	Bobby Womack

'Just Can't Give You Up'   Mystique Merlin

'Casonova'   Coffee

Then I placed Lorna's CD in the CD player and set up the track 'Distant Lovers' by Marvin Gaye as I described to Graham and the girls what it was like to see Marvin Gaye live.

"I was sitting in the Royal Albert Hall with my mate Debbie Mcquire, when Marvin Gaye walked out on the stage wearing a Levi type jacket, pair of jeans, a massive pair of silver boots and a red beany hat. The crowd went absolutely mad, then when Marvin Gaye sang 'Distant Lovers' it sounded something like this." I pressed the start button on the small CD player and tweaked up the volume. Once the song kicked in, all four listened in amazement. I started strolling round the room with a spoon for a mike, trying to show my chalet mates the feeling that Marvin Gaye puts into every word that he sings.

When the record finished little Emma said, "Reggie you ought to be on the stage mate, no way do you look like Marvin Gaye but that was brilliant."

"Yeah alright Emm, now I know you're taking the pee."

Then Emma said, "I want you to make me a CD of all the records you've played me. Your impression of Marvin Gaye was brill but the record I liked the most was 'Daylight' by Bobby Womack—it seems like it's the story of my life. Bobby Womack is one of your favourite artists isn't he Reg? I quite like some of his material myself but that sound 'Daylight' is something else."

"Yeah I know what you mean Emma, it's got everything, even a birds chorus in the middle of the record."

Those of you who haven't heard 'Daylight' by Bobby Womack just go and buy it! The lyrics are something like: ...and it looks like daylight's/ gonna catch me up again/ most people like getting up/ when I'm just getting in... Then the 'choon' fades and finishes, the lyrics just about sums up most of our lives as Soulies. I know that most of us dance to the beats of the 'choons' we are hearing, but if the beat is too fast or not to your liking, try dancing to the lyrics sometimes. You can give a better interpretation to what you are hearing by dancing to different parts of the sound that you are listening too.

Another amusing part of this particular Caister weekender was when we all went out, as the three girls were all so good looking, stunning in fact, we got the nickname of Charlie and his Angels. Even when I went swimming, some of the black fellows would say, "Hey Chalkie Charlie. Where are your angels?"

I would just reply, "They're all still in bed mate but they will all be out tonight."

Once you get to know most of the Caister bunch, it's a laugh a minute and this is what makes these weekends so special, especially when there's a nice crew of Soulies in the same caravan. All I've got to do now is try and persuade me old mate Yogi to attend some of the Caister Soul weekenders.

Midway through the following week, just as Karen had predicted, Simon Clark phoned me up and said, "All of your artwork is finished on your scooter panels. But if I were you I would leave it till the weekend, it will give the lacquer a chance to harden." So that's exactly what I did. I picked up the panels with my brother Geoff on the following Sunday.

Once I'd got them back from Colchester, I laid all the panels out in the front room of my little cottage and they looked absolutely brilliant. Over the next four weeks, I managed to finish the scooter. It passed the MOT but on the way back from the MOT centre, the scooter kept slipping out of third gear and as I had no idea what was wrong, I thought I'd better phone a professional. So, I scanned through the phone book for Roger Knox's phone number. Roger is one of the older members of our scooter club and has owned scooters all his life, so in my reckoning this makes Roger a professional scooter mechanic. Roger is just like Peter Mullinger, so enthusiastic, and between them what they didn't know about how scooters work, wasn't worth knowing.

As soon as I told Roger what the problem was, he said, "I'll be round straight away," and in no time at all he was knocking on my workshop door. But instead of looking at the gears, his eyes looked straight at the clutch, he fiddled with the clutch cable and then the gear cables.

"Right Reg, what's wrong here is all the cables are too tight, we'll sort the gear cables out first as there is plenty of adjustment on the adjusters."

Once we had slackened off the gear cables we looked at the clutch cable and this was a totally different matter.

Roger said, "There's no more adjustment left on the clutch cable adjuster and also the inner cable is too short, what we'll have to do is shorten the outer cable. To save taking it all out, we'll have to cut it in situ but whatever you do don't damage the inner cable. We'll shorten the cable from the head set."

Once we had disconnected the clutch cable from the clutch lever. Roger cut about an inch off the plastic sheathing. Then whilst Roger held the cable with some pliers, I cut away the outer cable reinforcement using a hack saw, a job which would have taken at least half a day by myself was all complete within the hour. The scooter was running perfectly with two weeks to go before Christmas.

The reason I desperately wanted the scooter before Christmas was so that I could drive it around to the house in Leverstock Green, where the first owner on the logbook Mr Alexander lived. One of Mr Alexander's daughters called Sue was over from the States for the holiday period. His other daughter Jackie knew that I had the scooter all along, but as it was in such a bad condition, we didn't hold out much hope of me ever completing the job. So, she didn't let her family know that I had the scooter, but as you all know I did complete it.

On the day I was taking it round to Mr Alexander's house, my first port of call was Jackie's house. I parked the scooter behind her husband Russell's van, out of sight of their front door. Then I went and knocked on the door which Russell answered he said, "Hello Reg long time no see, come in I'll put the kettle on. To what do we owe this privilege?"

I then said, "Well Russell about two years ago I saw you in the Red Lion pub in Apsley."

"Oh yeah, I remember, weren't you doing up an old LD?"

"Yes I was, and you said at the time that you had just sold one and that you had wished that you had let me have it. But what you didn't know was the scooter I was doing up, was the one that you had sold to Paul Tooley."

Russell answered with, "No—you're joking me."

Just at that moment, Jackie walked into the kitchen and said, "Hi Reg have you got the scooter with you?"

Russell piped up with, "You knew about this all the time?"

Jackie said, "I've known about it for a couple of years."

Russell passed me my cup of tea and said, "Have you changed it much?"

"Only the colour, mate; from red and cream to beige and cream, and the scooter is now called 'Café Latte'."

"I'll put my shoes on, I've got to see this."

Whilst Russell was looking for his shoes, Jackie said, "Did you manage to get the brown and cream gingham table cloth for the picnic basket Reg?"

"Yeah, I had to make the table cloth on my sewing machine. I bought the cloth in Watford market, it weren't 'arf hard to get brown and cream gingham, I really wanted half-inch squares but as it was so hard to come by, the three-eighths will have to do."

"Right," said Russ. We walked outside to where the scooter was parked. As soon as Russell laid his eyes on it, his words were, "It's unbelievable—look at it. Who did the airbrushing? The colours are perfect."

It was like a kid getting a late Christmas present, which he really wanted and didn't get in the first place. He was strutting around the scooter like an old chicken taking pictures on his mobile phone. After about twenty minutes, Jackie, Russell and I headed around to Jackie's dad's house as it was only in the next road. Jackie and Russ were walking and I was riding alongside them.

All Russ kept saying was, "I don't believe it," until Jackie said, "Russell, you sound like Victor Meldrew off the telly."

When we arrived at Mr Alexander's house, the only one who was in, was Sue.

Her first words were, "Hello Reg, is that your new scooter? My dad had one just like it. Jackie and I used to play on it when we were kids."

It was at that point that Jackie said, "You'd better have a closer look at it Sue."

Then Sue gave that look of astonishment and said, "That's never dad's old bike. Oh my God. It is, isn't it?"

Jackie gave a cheeky grin, nodded her head and said, "Put your shoes on and come and have a closer look."

After about twenty minutes, Jackie and I were getting the same reaction that we did when Russell first saw the scooter.

Sue said, "Dad's not here at the moment but he won't be long."

"Go and put the kettle on Sue," said Russell, "while me and Reg park the scooter in the back garden where your dad used to leave it. We'll have a cup of tea and wait in the kitchen till he gets back."

Then whilst we were chatting and drinking our tea we noticed the light shining through the side door of Jackie's dad's garage and Sue said, "He's here, watch for his reaction."

Mr Alexander took one step into his back garden and knew instantly the bike was his old scooter. He was so pleased to see that it was still alive, he had to touch it to make sure it wasn't a mirage.

I said, "I was a bit worried that you would be upset that I had changed the colour."

"No, not at all Reg it's perfect. I love your theme as well. I had no idea I would see my scooter again, especially in this condition." So, taken aback by the whole affair, Mr Alexander disappeared for a few minutes. When he returned he was holding an old photo album and gave me a photo of his late wife sitting on his scooter in a fifties style skirt and an old fashioned type cardigan.

In the background, there appeared to be some old steam train signals. I asked Mr Alexander when the photo was taken; his reply was the year he bought the scooter in 1957. I then pointed to a small hole in the floorboards and asked why it was there.

Mr Alexander looked down and sighed, "I had the scooter most of my life and when I was getting older I started to get arthritis in my hand. I couldn't flick the dip switch with my thumb, so I fitted a dip switch on the floor to operate the lights with my foot."

These comments summed up the feeling I was having of this man and his family, as I said goodbye I felt so pleased that I had made them all so happy and all I did was restore the man's scooter.

As for the rest of Christmas, it wasn't too bad really, my family knew that we were going to struggle a bit as this was the first Christmas without Mother but all in all we coped okay. I had some wonderful pressies, my son Jack and daughter Holly bought me a couple of DJ record boxes for singles. My sister Jackie bought me a DJ box for LPs and you got a little light with it so you can see what you're doing when you're playing your sounds. It seems as if they are pointing me in the direction of buying some more records. Hmmm I wonder.....

And then we came to the present that I bought Yogi, it was a present that didn't only blow Yogi away, it blew me away as well. Prior to the Christmas holidays, I was working in my workshop at the back of my garden. Although I love working in the workshop, I'm always on my own. It can be quite a lonely place and when your head isn't full of calculations through making something for a client, you find that you have a lot of thinking time. Just recently I've been thinking about all the concerts that Yogi and I had the privilege of going to. Also all of the brilliant Soul singers that we have both seen, we saw them in the prime time of their careers. Although sometimes I hear of the odd concert or show being advertised where one of our idols from the past are performing, I have had the tendency to avoid going to see any of them, mainly because I wouldn't like to see them struggle with some of the high notes that their voices used to reach. I want to remember how good they were in their prime. The only way you can revitalise these memories is when you hear one of their 'choons' on your wireless.

There's been many a time when Yogi and I have been travelling to a do and a certain 'choon' starts playing. Within a few seconds one of us would say, "Do you remember when?" and all of a sudden we are both reliving the concert in question. On this particular Friday afternoon, my thoughts were disturbed by one of my neighbours wanting to see how I was getting on with my scooter. When the chap had left, for a bit of company I stuck my workshop wireless on. It's one of those posh digital DAB things. The station, which the wireless is mostly set to, is 102.2 Smooth FM. It only gets switched to the Five Live sports channel if Liverpool are playing, or I want to know the football results. Otherwise it's 102.2 Smooth FM. So on this particular day, I was attempting to sing along to 'Tripping On Your Love' with Kenny Thomas, when the record was cut short by the announcement of a *David Gest Soul Spectacular Show* at the Cadogan Hall, London.

Live in concert were to be:

Peabo Bryson, Russell Tompkins Jr and The New Stylistics, Bonnie Tyler, Martha Reeves and The Vandellas, Candi Staton, Denise Williams, Billy Paul, Freda Payne, Dorothy Moore, Carl Carlton and William Bell.

I jotted the ticket line number down on a piece of wood and thought to myself 'what a line up! That will do nicely.' After locking up my workshop, I made the all important phone call to our Lorraine, Yogi's wife to make sure that Yogi is available for the dates given and once I got the all clear, I said to Lorraine, "I'll let you know if I manage to get the tickets."

I called out to Debbie and asked her to read out the phone number written on the piece of wood sat on the dining room table. I managed to get through straight away and as the gentleman was about to tell me the various prices of the tickets. I said, "I'm not interested in what the tickets cost, I just want two of the best seats in the house for me and a special mate of mine."

A few minutes later I phoned back Lorraine to let her know that it was all sorted and I gave her the date of the concert. Shortly after putting the phone down, I fired up my laptop and printed off the line-up of all the artists that we were going to see. I stuck the print out in a Christmas card saying 'Happy Christmas Mate, we're going to a concert,' then I nipped up to where Yogi lives and left the card on Lorraine's kitchen worktop.

Lorraine said, "Reg he will be over the moon, mate. Russell Tompkins JR is one of his favourites and he still goes on about the time you went to see the Stylistics in Ipswich."

"I know he does Lorraine. I just hope that all the artists we're going to see are just as good as they were when we were kids. I'll see you soon, any problems tell him to give me a ring."

The next day Yogi phoned me up and just said, "Excellent, thanks very much, what a line-up, I can't wait."

On the night of the concert, Yogi picked me up and off we set. When we arrive at the Cadogan Hall, there was a parking space right outside the main door, which I thought was left for the arrival of the stretch limos but no, the stretch limos didn't stand a chance because that's where Yogi wanted to park his car. And, after a few minutes wait, that's exactly where Yogi parked his car, right outside the main entrance. Whilst Yogi was parking, I quickly jumped out the car because Russell Tompkins JR was signing some autographs by a small side door of the venue. There were about four or five people gathered around Russell, so I waited for my turn and he signed the complimentary slip of paper, which was in the envelope with the tickets. I had a little chat with the man and he seemed like a really nice guy, then as Yogi and I had a bit of time to kill we went for a drink in a small bar not far from the venue in Sloane Square. We did have a laugh; I told Yogi we were in a gay bar. His reply was, "Why do you think I'm standing with my back against the wall, hey look there's one over there with his eye on you Reg." "

"Yeah all right Yogi," I replied.

After about an hour we made our way back to the Cadogan Hall and as we were about to enter the place I said to Yogi, "I wonder who owns that posh car in front of the main door?"

He chirped up with, "Probably one of the artists or someone really special."

Once we got inside the foyer, the place was dead smart. There was a big round drinks bar right in the middle of the high ceiling room selling champagne, wine and various beers. Also a small table was set up selling CDs and programmes. This place was a massive change to Camden's Roundhouse or the Finsbury Park Rainbow where we used to see our favourite Soul singers perform.

As we were making our way to where we were going to sit, I passed Yogi his ticket and this is where I got told off, "You never paid this much Reg?"

"Well Yogi, I reckon we've got about twenty to thirty years left Souling together, so there's still plenty of time."

Yogi's reply was, "We might have about twenty to thirty years left but they don't. Your old mate James Brown died on Christmas Day, didn't he?"

"Yeah, I suppose so mate,"

We both passed our tickets to the ticket clipper and the young lady said, "Six rows down, eight seats in on your left."

We took our seats and the view was second to none. You could only be in awe of the place; it wasn't dissimilar to a modern church. At the back of the stage, there was a high shaped arch and the sound of the background music was nice and clear so the acoustics of this place were very good. Then as the night went on every artist sounded as good as his or her records. Our favourites were The Stylistics and Billy Paul but that wasn't to say the others weren't as good 'cos they were they were all marvellous and gave a brilliant account of what they were all about in their day.

Whether it was Dorothy Moore's 'Misty Blue', Candi Staton's 'Young Hearts Run Free' or the Denise Williams' ballad 'Free'. I'm getting tingles across my shoulders and down my arms just thinking about it all to be quite honest. Thinking about it, it had to be the best concert I'd ever been to, as there were so many different artists appearing on the same night. Yep. I believe David Gest got it exactly right. His selection of singers was absolutely perfect.

As we left the venue Yogi said, "We're gonna be hard pushed to better that Reg, I loved it, I won't forget this night in a hurry. Thanks very much, it was one of the best pressies I've ever had."

Whilst we were travelling back all of a sudden, Yogi pulled over in the middle of the West End at another exclusive Yogi parking place. "Right Reg, out you get."

Yogi locked the car and we walked to Argyle Street. "What do you fancy mate? We can have a Steak, Italian, Greek or whatever you like."

"I fancy a steak Yogi."

"Right then, steak it is." This was a perfect way to end a perfect Soulful evening out.

Whilst we were eating our meal, Yogi and I agreed that after the concert we had both witnessed, instead of shying away from these shows when some of our favourite artists are appearing, we will take the chance and go and see them perform. You never know they might be similar to a vintage bottle of wine, the older they get the better they are.

It wasn't until a few days later when I was sitting in my living room talking to my wife Debbie, telling her just how good the *David Gest Soul Show* was when she replied, "That's good because you're going to another one, here's the other half of your Christmas present."

I undid the envelope that Debbie placed in my hand and there were two tickets for the Tamla Motown Show called *Dancing in the Streets* at the London Playhouse Theatre on the Embankment. Then Debbie says to my amazement, "I'm coming with you." Well I couldn't believe my ears, the thoughts running through my mind were, 'Have all my dreams come true? Is my lovely wife becoming a Soulie? Could this be the first of many or just a flash in the pan?' Whatever the outcome, the fact of the matter is I was going to a Soul show with my wife Debbie and that was good enough for me.

When the day of the show arrived, Debbie and I decided to leave Apsley Station around about five o'clock, get up to town early, so we could have a meal before the show. We looked around the West End and ended up in the same Angus Steak House that Yogi had taken me to a few days before. Although the meal was lovely, if I had known what I was about to find out, I reckon we should have travelled straight to the Embankment Station. The theatre where the show was being held was right by the London Eye alongside the river Thames. On the Thames were some quite large boats moored up which anyone could walk on as they were licensed restaurants. Debbie and I walked on to one of these boats and had a drink, whilst we were on board we noticed that the meals looked rather nice. So if ever we're going to a show in this area again we will definitely dine on one of these boats. It will make a nice change.

When we entered the theatre, I thought, 'Wow, I've been to two of the most amazing little venues in a week.' The London Playhouse Theatre was yet another tidy little place, this time with a drinks bar downstairs from the main foyer. When Debbie and I had taken our seats, we were very pleased with our view of the stage. But unbeknown to us, the view wasn't going to be a major issue on this occasion, as twenty minutes into the show everyone was standing, dancing and clapping hence the title of the show *Dancing in the Streets*. This show was truly a brilliant celebration of the Motown sound from days gone by. The professional singers who were picked to portray the original artists that we all loved captured the Motown sound. They were pretty near the mark, but not perfect, as it must be a tall order to even contemplate trying to sing like Stevie Wonder, Marvin Gaye, Diana Ross etc.

Whilst listening to the various songs I must admit some of them were the same as the originals, but by the time the show was coming to an end, I started to realise just how good our all time favourites really were with their range of vocals. Also through going to this show, I am finding I'm having the tendency to disagree with the comments made in the film *Standing in the Shadows of Motown*—the Story of the Funk Brothers. As one of the chaps said, "The background musicians were so good even Deputy Dawg could have sung in front of them." No, I don't think so. In my opinion after going to this show the Motown sound was a mixing bowl of brilliant singers, brilliant musicians and brilliant songwriters, it was a combined effort, everyone needed each other to create the music, which became the Motown sound. If you are an avid Motown fan, this show is well worth a visit. A great night of singing and dancing with a trip down memory lane, well worth checking out, I loved it.

The next day I was sitting in my garden talking to me Mum about the show. Now I know what you're all thinking I'm going off my rocker, but let me explain. Two months after Mum passed away my Dad strolled down the garden path with a small bag and says. "Here you go Reg, here's some of your Mum's ashes; we've all had some. Jackie and Geoff have got some, I've got some, some are scattered by her Mum and Dad up the crematorium and some are by her caravan in Yarmouth. She's been to more places dead than when she was alive."

"Cheers Dad, I'll do something special with them."

So what I did with mine was, I built a little brick stand with a paving slab on the top, inside the stand are Mum's ashes. Then I placed a decorative fountain on top of the slab, wired it all up with an outside switch on my garden fence. So, if I am sitting or working in the garden I can flick the old switch on and have a chat with my mother.

On this particular occasion I said, "Alright Mum? How are we today then? I had a great night last night and I only went Souling with Debbie. No I did Mum, I'm not having you on." (I'm inclined to keep these conversations pretty brief, as I don't want the neighbours thinking I have lost the plot).

After keeping mum updated on my latest excursion, I was sitting on my garden seat and looking at the pictures in the newspaper. I scanned through the telly page and noticed a programme called *Soul Britannia*. I wasn't going Souling that night so I thought it could be well worth a spec. The period when the programme started was about ten years before my book. I found my mind being torn between wishing I was born earlier, rather than I was in 1954. If I'd been born in 1944, I would have been present right from the start of this evolution of Soul music in England; however, on the other hand, would I still be going to all-nighters at sixty-three? Who knows? At this present day, I'm fifty-three still lasting the whole night and giving a good account of myself on the dance floor. I just wish I'd been slightly older than I was when my Uncle Jack Mahoney invited our family to the Yankie Air base at Ruislip. You see, Uncle Jack was a pilot in the American Air Force, but after being shot down in 'Nam, he was put in charge of the control tower. The year was around 1962 and I was eight years old. If I had been eighteen, I would have been of an age to pay more attention to the record titles in the jukebox rather than just looking at the flashing lights and all the water moving round in a decorative tubing, whilst sipping on the best milk shake I had ever had in my life. I wondered why just by driving through a pair of military style gates our family entered such a different way of living. Then as my thoughts faded and the telly programme progressed,

I thought, 'Oh no. Someone has only made a documentary of my book and it hasn't even been published yet'—wishful thinking eh?

The following day I went to measure up a staircase job for one of my skiing mates, Andy Ferguson, who lived in Leighton Buzzard. Whilst driving, my mobile rang, so I pulled over onto the hard shoulder to take the call and it was my mate Alan Cottee.

He said, "You're gonna love me son, did you see the *Soul Britannia* programme last night?"

"Yeah I did, why?"

"Well what are you doing on Sunday night? I've only gone and got two tickets for a concert which is linked to the programme and we're gonna see Sam Moore out of Sam and Dave, Eddie Floyd, Gino Washington, Jimmy James, Eric Burden and one of your favourites Madeline Bell—what do you think?"

"Yeah mate, how much?"

"It's twenty five pound and it's going to be held at the Barbican. I'll drive."

"What time do you want me ready?"

"Be ready to go about five o'clock Reg."

"Brilliant Alan, I'll look forward to it, you say Madeline Bell is singing too?"

"Yes she is mate."

I really like seeing some of the artistes that have had success on the northern scene, but they never seem to sing their Northern records live. I thought I bet she doesn't sing 'Picture Me Gone' just like if you go and see Terry Caller you won't hear him sing 'Ordinary Joe' or would you ever hear the Pointer Sisters singing 'Send Him Back'? No I don't think so. Then I started thinking I haven't been to a concert in about fifteen years then all of a sudden, I go to three in six weeks.

On the night of the show every singer who appeared, sang beyond all my expectations. My favourite on the night was Sam Moore until Madeline Bell said, "Now here's one for all my Northern Soul friends", you guessed it, she only sang 'Picture Me Gone' and it was perfection. My ears had never been so spoilt. After visiting these recent concerts, it seems to me that I've now only got to visit a Jazz club, maybe the Jazz

Café in Camden. Or, something that I would really like to do is to go back to Ronnie Scott's one evening. Then once more my love for Soul music would have taken me full circle, as it did twenty-odd years ago and I'm still loving every minute of it.

SO WHERE DO WE GO FROM HERE?

Who knows what life has in store for us?

The different types of Soul music could not be closer, as I have said before at the Caister Soul weekenders, nowadays they even dedicate at least six hours to the Northern Soul scene. I've met countless friends over the last seven years and life couldn't be richer.

I fully expect Yogi and I to be Souling well into our vintage years, but as for now the first fifty-odd have been awesome and long may they continue. In the last seven years, did I ever capture that special moment from the past? You bet your life I did. It was when Yogi played 'Game Players' by Dooley Silverspoon at the Bennetts End Soul Club and for three minutes fifty four seconds, I was back on that sprung loaded floor in Wigan Casino.

Afterword

Searching for Soul and Finding It

Searching For Soul is obviously about Yogi and I looking through count-less record boxes, whether they were in the basements of music shops, record stores, market stalls or privately owned boxes by Soulies on the Wigan balcony. We even found some records in the odd antique shop. All the time we were Searching For Soul.

We always dreamed of going to America to buy our music; we haven't made it yet but if we do ever get there, I can just imagine an old chap sitting in his small record shop saying: "If you want that kind of music son, you should go to England, as most of it is stored safely away in private record collections. That's where all the Soul music is nowadays; we don't have any left in America any more." And you know what's so ironic, he may be right—we've bought it all!

Or, was *Searching For Soul* about growing up through these special years? The times and places; sharing your parents' anguish in the early days, as they struggled on through life, so that us kids could become what we are today. In my case, however hard my Mum and Dad had to work, we always had a holiday, even if it was just a coach trip to Southend. A day at the seaside made all the difference.

Or, could *Searching For Soul* have been about the fashions and the clothes or the way we were in our teenage years, going around as a unit and feeling that you were never on your own? You were part of a movement whether you were Mods, Skinheads or just a bunch of cool dudes out for a laugh and sharing each others' company, which is at its best when some of us are having a bad time. The way we rally round when some of us are in trouble or when someone has lost someone they love—a member of family or when you break up with a boy or girl-friend, it's all a grieving process, which is made easier when you have the experiences of feeling each other's pain; a skill, which I believe, came from listening to the lyrics of the songs that had been written, by people probably in the same boat.

Or was *Searching For Soul* the way some of us supported our designated football clubs with such passion it was like a religion; then our own off springs followed suit through the faith of their fathers? Is this what searching for soul is all about?

Or could *Searching For Soul* have been the first time we tapped our feet to the beat of a record, which then turned into dance steps? There was that feeling that rose from deep inside your stomach and touched your Soul. The tingles that ran down your arms as soon as you had discovered what kind of message the Soul singer was trying to get over to you. You know what I am trying to say to you all—if you're a true Soul fan, you've all been there. However the music has touched you and affected your lives, it's a passion that will stay with you for the rest of your days.

Searching for soul and finding it?

Yes I did.

I found it—I found it in

You, the people.

Acknowledgements

At this point, I'd like to thank my lovely wife Debbie for putting up with me, my sister Jackie and my wonderful friend Alison Parkes for their tremendous support and encouragement with my story. Also my mate Yogi for sharing all these experiences with me,

Last, but not least, all you Soulies—the best people in the world. Friendships that can't be measured.

Anyone can love someone, but this is a darn sight more than that.

'We're Just Ordinary People': inspiring words from John Legend.

I love you all,
all the best,
Reg.

Appendices

TOP TEN FAVOURITE VENUES FROM THE PAST

1. Wigan Casino — Wigan
2. California Ballroom — Dunstable
3. Catacombs — Wolverhampton
4. Bali Hi — Margate
5. Ronnie Scott's — Frith Street, London
6. Cleethorpes Pier — Cleethorpes
7. Cherry Trees — Welwyn Garden City
8. Top Rank — Watford
9. Goldmine — Canvey Island
10. Village Bowl — Bournemouth

TOP TEN FAVOURITE VENUES FROM THE PRESENT

1. Denton Café (Beach End Of Pier) — Worthing
2. Kings Hall — Stoke
3. The Ritz — Desborough
4. Cadogan Hall — London
5. Plinston Hall — Letchworth
6. The Railway Club — Peterborough
7. Hemel Town FC. — Hemel Hempstead
8. Barbican Centre — London
9. Bisley Pavilion — Bisley Barracks
10. Rising Sun — Southgate

TOP TEN FAVOURITE DJ'S FROM THE PAST

1. Richard Searling   Wigan Casino

2. Brucie Benson   California Ballroom

3. Robbie Vincent   Radio London

4. Pep   Catacombs

5. Kev Roberts   Wigan Casino

6. Greg Edwards   Jazz FM.

7. Soul Shep   Village Bowl, Bournemouth

8. Chris Hill   Goldmine / Caister

9. Rocky Rivers   Bennetts End Youth Club

10. Russ Winstanley   Wigan Casino

TOP TEN FAVOURITE DJ'S FROM THE PRESENT

1. Kev Laws   Norwich

2. Arthur Fenn   Selby, Yorkshire

3. Taffy Guy   Plinston/southgate

4. Yogi (Paul Bohknecht)   Sounds Of Soul

5. Pete Collins   Caister/Vevo's

6. Soul Sam   Wrexham

7. Maggot (Tony Matthews)   Caister

8. Ronnie O'brian   Solar Radio/Caister

9. Molly   Bedford

10. Shaun Chapman   Talk Of The South

LATEST RECORDS PURCHASED 2006/2007

1. Funny How We Changed Places

Dee Dee Warwick

Label: Private Stock

2. Overdose Of Joy

Eugene Record

Label: Warner Bros. Promo

3. Just Say Goodbye

Esther Philips

Label; English Atlantic

4. Raindrops Love And Sunshine

Robert John

Label: AGM

5. Let Me Try

The Odds & Ends

Label: Today

6. Nobody But You

Esther Philips

Label: Roulette

7. No One There

Martha Reeves & The Vandellas

Label: English Motown

8. My Life

Chanelle

Label: Sold Out

9. Just Be Thankful

Omar & Angie Stone

Label: Studio

10. Searching

Change

Label Wea

11. Girl You're Too Young

Archie Bell & The Drells

Label: Us Atlantic

12. Groovy People

          Lou Rawls

          Label: Phillidelphia Demo

13. Let Me Make Love To You

          Gene Chandler

          Label: 20th Century

14. I Can Tell

          Ed Summers

          Label: Soya

15. Just A Kiss Away

          Buddy Miles

          Label: Columbia

16. Too Late

          Mandrill

          Label: Arista

17. Ordinary Joe

          Terry Callier

          Label: Elektra

18. That's When The Tears Start

          Blossoms

          Label: Reprise

19. Making My Daydream Real

          We The People

          Label: Lion

20. Ordinary People

          John Legend

          Label: Su

21. My Good Friend

          James Pioneers

          Label: Mercury

22. I Can't Stop The Rain

          David Ruffin

          Label: Motown

TOP FIVE FAVOURITE RECORD DEALERS

1. THE SOULMINE
    ROOM 1 FIRST FLOOR
    16 GROSVENOR ROAD
    ALDERSHOT GU11 1DP ENGLAND
    Website: www.thesoulminelimited.com

2. SOUL BOWL RECORDS
    P.O. BOX 3
    KINGS LYNN NORFOLK
    PE32 IYG ENGLAND
    email: soulbowl1@aol.com

3. CRAZY BEAT RECORDS
    87 CORBETS TEY ROAD
    UPMINSTER.
    ESSEX RM14 2AH ENGLAND
    email: sales@crazybeat.co.uk

4. SOUL BROTHER RECORDS
    1 KESWICK ROAD
    EAST PUTNEY
    LONDON SW15 2HL ENGLAND
    Email: soulbrothers@soulbrother.com

5. CHAPMAN RECORDS SEAN CHAPMAN
    13 HEAL LODWIG
    CHURCH VILLAGE
    PONTYPRIDD
    CF38 ITJ WALES
    Website: www.chapmanrecords.co.uk

ABOUT THE AUTHOR

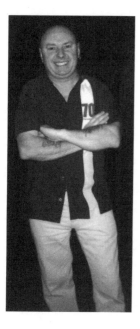

'Reg' is now in his mid- fifties, a carpenter by trade working for himself. His passion for wood and working with his hands is more than matched by his love of Liverpool FC and music. A strong family man, married to Debbie for over 20 years, he idolises his daughter Holly and son Jack. Reg is now head of the family as the eldest of three children to Dad Ray and Mum Colleen.

Born in 1954 in Hemel Hempstead, Hertfordshire he has lived there all his life; well, so far anyway. Reg left school at 14 with no academic qualifications, but an appreciation of wood and a craftsman's eye to create beautiful pieces of furniture. Having struggled to read and write, he fell into the carpentry trade to, in his words, " to earn a shilling".

Reg grew up through many changing eras and during his life he has encountered many styles, fads, fashions, haircuts and much more. Still very active in his enjoyment of Soul, Reg recently found the scooter scene and now has not one, but two scooters, a Lambretta and a Vespa; both vintage models.

Reg's philosophy on life is: "you only get out of life what you put in" and Reg puts a great deal in. Never without a supportive word or a smile, Reg gives of himself to others, offering a shoulder to cry on, an ear for anyone to bend or a story of one of his many life experiences. Reg's current nickname is 'the biggest smile on the dance floor' and there's not many that would disagree with that.

saf publishing

www.safpublishing.co.uk

info@safpublishing.co.uk